Bumblebee
ˈbʌmb(ə)lbiː/
noun
A large, hairy, social bee.
With its heavy body
and tiny wings, it seems
the bumblebee should
not be able to fly –
yet it does so with
grace and efficiency.

For Annika

Bumblebee Nation
The hidden story of the new Swedish model

BY DAVID CROUCH

KARL-ADAM BONNIERS STIFTELSE

© **KABS 2018**
Karl-Adam Bonniers Stiftelse
© Text: David Crouch
© Photography: Tina Axelsson
Other photos: TT Nyhetsbyrån page 7, 71, 74,
Sara Franck page 161, Volvo cars page 196.
Editor in chief: Mats Bergstrand
Deputy editor: Heather Farmbrough
Graphic design: Mikael Engblom 2dd
Print: Joma Grafisk Produktion, Sweden.
This book is produced in Sweden and printed
on Swedish paper from Iggesund and Mölndal.

ISBN: 978-91-983763-2-6

CONTENTS

INTRODUCTION:
AND YET IT FLIES

In the late summer of 2015, I started a Chinese whisper that went around the world and reinforced the prejudices held by tens of millions of people about Scandinavia.

It began with the best of intentions. I was still new to Sweden, where I had started out as a freelance reporter after many years of comfortable desk jobs in London. I thought I had discovered a good story, so on a sunny August morning I set off to investigate.

My friend Daniel, a photojournalist and out-doors enthusiast, picked me up in his battered Volvo estate, which was normally full of mountain bikes, surf-boards or rock-climbing equipment. We drove across the Älvsborg suspension bridge at the mouth of the river as the sun shone on its playful, egg-shell green girders. Towards the horizon, a line of vast wind turbines revolved slowly, perched among dark knuckles of rock where the granite coast crumbles into the sea. This was Gothenburg, Sweden's second city and now my home.

We pulled up on a leafy cul-de-sac among the tall birches that surround Svartedalen retirement home, a red brick block in an area better known for its poverty and gang violence. I got out my notepad and Daniel his camera. This unlikely setting was an experiment in the future of work. For the past six months, the elderly care nurses had been working a six-hour day, instead of the usual eight, for the same wage.

Since the 1990s, Svartedalen had been facing more work with fewer and fewer staff. "We can't do it any more," said Ann-Charlotte Dahlbom Larsson,

who ran the home. "There is a lot of illness and depression among staff in the care sector because of exhaustion, the lack of balance between work and life is not good for anyone." Already, she said, on the six-hour day staff were feeling noticeably better, but the standard of care had also improved. The new arrangement was likely to be more expensive – the home had hired extra nurses to cover the gaps left by the shorter working hours.

Lise-Lotte Pettersson, an assistant nurse, showed us around, taking a moment along the way to dance tenderly with an elderly man. Caring for the residents, some of whom had dementia, demanded constant vigilance and creativity, and with a six-hour day Lise-Lotte could sustain a higher standard of care, she said:

"I used to be exhausted all the time, I would come home from work and pass out on the sofa. But not now. I am much more alert: I have much more energy for my work, and also for family life."

I first learned about this experiment from a political flyer stuck to the wall of a tram stop near our flat. The country was preparing for an election, and with the help of Google Translate I was trying to understand what was going on. A bleak and soulless street corner opposite the cemetery, with its injunction to "Think about Death" inscribed over the gates, seemed like an dismal place for a declaration about the future of humanity, but there it was: something called the Left Party, whoever they were, wanted a 6-hour working day. I wanted to be on a beach in the Bahamas, but there was about an equal chance of either of those things happening, I thought. And I got on the tram.

But somehow, here in this wet and windy city on the northern edge of the planet, the idea found a hearing. Gothenburg city council, run by the centre-left Social Democrats who have dominated Swedish politics since the 1930s, agreed to a small experiment at the nursing home. Meanwhile, on the other side of the city, a Toyota servicing centre had moved to a 6-hour day more than a decade ago, leading to lower staff turnover, more efficient use of the machines and lower capital costs. I trawled the web and found a couple of small businesses that were also using a shorter working day, and bingo! I had something to sell – the stuff of freelance journalism.

The resulting piece was a hit with editors and readers of the *Guardian*, the British liberal daily that seemed happy to get an occasional bit of "good news" from Scandinavia with which to lighten up its coverage of grim events elsewhere. Sweden itself was about to turn into a much more urgent international story, as the country opened its doors during the coming months to

160,000 refugees from the wars in Asia, Africa and the Middle East.

However the genie was out of the bottle. It turned out that my feature about Lise-Lotte and some Toyota mechanics appealed to every prejudice that we hold about Sweden, the land of Abba and IKEA, of blonde hair and blue eyes, of sex and socialism and Scandi silliness. Scotland was the first to take notice. Columnist Robert McNeil wrote in the *Herald* newspaper:

"What have these wacky Scandinavians been up to now? I will tell you what: experimenting with a six-hour working day, that's what. A typical Britisher will think: 'Six-hour working day? That's immoral. First, it was pornography. Now this. The Scandinavians need reining in.' ... We cannot believe every-thing they do in Scandinavia is good and everything we do is bad, despite all the evidence. But it's nice to have a beacon of hope, however illusory. And the thought that somebody somewhere is trying to organise society on sane lines gives us courage to carry on in Barmy Britannia."

During the Cold War, the idea that things could be different, that society could be organised along alternative lines, was often connected to Russia. But after the Soviet monolith collapsed, we were left with... Sweden. The story spread like wildfire. Ireland was next. "Businesses across Sweden are moving towards a six-hour working day to improve work-life balance," declared the Irish *Examiner*; the Irish *Mirror* wrote that the trial of a six-hour working day in one of Europe's richest countries "threatens to revolutionise the lives of millions of people". Already, in the hands of editors keen not to let facts stand in the way of a good story, three businesses and a nursing home had become "business-es across Sweden" and a revolution for the masses.

"Sweden is moving towards a standard 6-hour work day, with businesses across the country having already implemented the change," wrote *Science Alert*, referring to my story. The website of *The Independent*, a British news-paper, repeated the tale, citing *Science Alert*. The media echo chamber was in overdrive. The next day, *Britain's Daily Telegraph* headlined its story: "Why the UK should adopt Sweden's six-hour workday." *Fortune*, the magazine of US business, explained: "What the US could learn from Sweden's 6-hour work day". The *New York Times* sent a reporter to Gothenburg who produced a more sober article that was almost a carbon copy of mine, but it gave the story another big push into the Americas.

By then things had gone viral. It hit a breathless peak of nonsense almost exactly a year after my story first appeared, when the website *Smart Is The New Sexy* – motto: "We Love Science!" – issued a 40-second Facebook video montage of cheesy Swedish images, actually including a cheese fondue (N.B. that's Switzerland, not Sweden), which declared: "Sweden is officially moving to a six-hour working day." It was sent to me by an old school friend envious that fate had carried me to this blesséd haven. The last time I looked, that video had been viewed 42 million times.

So what became of the six-hour day in Sweden? As we might have expected, the experiment at Svartedalen came to a close in 2017. Short-term labour costs were up 20 per cent, while the gains were less tangible and quantifiable. The mountain of hype gave birth to a mouse. But the story of a Gothenburg nursing home spoke to our assumptions that in Scandinavia they do things differently, that work might not be just about growing the bottom line, and that a better, richer life might not be just a side-effect of the pursuit of profit, but something that can be planned for and worked towards. Could the "balance" between work and life – a juxtaposition that itself says so much about what work means to most of us – in fact be balanced towards life? And could work, instead of being an end in itself, the opposite of being out of work, become a means to a fuller life? Productivity in the industrialised world has doubled since the 1970s, so technically we have the potential for a much shorter working day, it's a question of how these productivity gains are distributed.

Like all prejudices, if you look only at the surface of things you can find evidence to back up any theory you like. And perhaps our assumptions about Scandinavia contain a speck of truth around which the pearl of myth has coalesced. I remember my first day at work in the journalism department at Gothenburg University. I left my office door ajar. Around 4pm I began to hear calls echoing down the corridor. Around 6pm I stepped out for a coffee to find the place deserted. The noises had been cries of "*Hej då!*", or goodbye, as staff went home just as I was settling down for a few more hours at my desk, as I had been accustomed to in London. You could be forgiven for thinking this was academia, where the work life balance might be taken to an extreme. In fact, as I was to find out to my own cost, Swedish universities are tough places to work, with high levels of stress and instability, and staff employed on rolling short-term contracts for years on end.

All the same, a working day of 8am to 4pm was observed by most university staff, including an hour for lunch, during which the doors to the building locked automatically, making it physically impossible for students – perish the thought – to disturb tutors during their break. The head of the department at the time also had a strategy of "management by fika", meaning that the twice daily breaks for coffee and buns, known as fika in Swedish, were useful opportunities for staff to share thoughts about their work, and to bond as a team.

10

And it seemed to work. At one of my part time jobs at a Swedish company in the city, my boss complained that she found it hard to get hold of senior management after 3 pm on Fridays because they were already on their boats.

To say anything meaningful about Sweden, however, we need to look below the surface. It is not enough for a journalist with a less than perfect grasp of Swedish to share some anecdotes about his adventures in a foreign land. And this, indeed, is the aim of this book – to talk to the people at the heart of the country's economy and find out what, if any, are the key features that make it distinctive. In a sense, every chapter is going to be looking at the world of work, because that is where the Swedish model stands or falls. Work is where the wealth is generated to pay for the shorter hours, the holidays, the parental leave, the welfare benefits, everything that constitutes Swedish society and which contributes to our visions of it – or perhaps, how we would like it to be. When people talk about the 35-hour working week in France, it is often in terms of how much damage it does to the economy. So is Sweden different? And if so, how? And why?

The person most responsible for popularising the notion that Sweden is unusual was the America journalist Marquis Childs. Childs came to Sweden in 1933 as a young man, and wrote a number of books, the best known of which was "Sweden: The Middle Way" (1936). He arrived in the country via Germany, which was gripped at the time by the Nazi takeover. To the east, Stalin's forced collectivisation had generated mass starvation, while the Kremlin was girding itself for the obscenity of the purges and the Gulag. At home, the US was in the depths of the Great Depression, from which there seemed no way out. The horrors of World War II were rapidly approaching. So the notion of a "middle way" between capitalism and socialism, "a spectacle of sanity and stability that other nations may study with profit", found a ready audience. Childs' book was a smash hit. His guiding metaphor added a new phrase to the political lexicon and led President Roosevelt to send a special commission to Europe to study cooperative methods. In one of the book's post-war editions, Childs wrote:

> *"It is perhaps this orderly surface of Swedish life that first attracts the visitor who comes from a world in which violent extremes contend for power, in a civilisation that must by comparison seem still amorphous."*

Today, the historical moment seems very different, in Europe at least. But there is still a whiff of the 1930s – the shockwaves of the 2008 financial crash, authoritarianism in the saddle in Moscow, Poland and Hungary, war in east

Ukraine, and parties on the far-right and left shaking the political establishment.

However, the book you are holding in your hands has no grand political ambitions, it makes no sweeping generalisations about capitalism versus socialism. It is a book of journalism, aiming to describe some modest truths about a spacious, peaceful country on the northernmost edge of Europe. It is a wealthy country, the economic powerhouse of Scandinavia. This is a book about how people are creating that wealth – the ultimate guarantor of peace and normality.

The guiding metaphor I have chosen is the bumblebee, an unpretentious insect that hums to itself as it works. According to the cliché, the bumblebee shouldn't be able to fly, it is too bulky and cumbersome, its wings comically small. Many aspects of Sweden suggest to the outsider that it shouldn't fly – the generous welfare system, the high average wages, its strong trade unions, the improbably long maternity leave, to name just a few. Göran Persson, a former prime minister of Sweden who will feature later in this book, said of his country:

"Think of a bumblebee. With its overly heavy body and little wings, it should not be able to fly – but it does. ... This is how so-called analysts view the Swedish economy. We 'defy gravity'. We have high taxes and a large public sector, and yet, Sweden reaches new heights. We are still flying, so well that many envy us for it today."

When I was first approached to write this book, my first reaction was to recommend other people who seemed better suited to the task. While I had lived in Sweden for three years, I was in no sense a Sweden expert, and didn't particularly like the place. It reminded me too much of Russia, where I had spent most of the 1990s, but with none of the romance. Having gone to great lengths to speak fluent Russian, the thought of similarly immersing myself in everything Swedish felt like an onerous task. I had abandoned a "good" job at the *Financial Times* in London to follow my Swedish girlfriend back to her home, and had only recently stopped regretting it.

On the other hand, the invitation came at a good time. I had spent a couple of happy years as one of the *Guardian's* go-to reporters for Scandinavia stories, and the paper seemingly couldn't get enough. I covered a hunt for a Russian submarines off Stockholm, women brewers in Gothenburg, the Julian Assange rape case, asylum and immigration, Sweden's hidden wine industry, moose hunting, the rise of the far right, developments in Finnish teaching and social care, even the Swedish passion for "drive-in bingo", much loved in the countryside on long summer evenings, where hundreds of people line their cars up in a field to play for small money prizes. I used to enjoy "checking my shares" – looking to see how many tens of thousands of times my articles had been shared on social media. One of my first viral hits concerned a sex-education cartoon for three-year-olds. Those Scandis, eh?! Typical. Whatever would they get up to next?

As a roving correspondent, writing also occasionally for the *Financial Times* and *New York Times*, I was like a pig in clover. I felt immensely fortunate – what a wonderful way to get to know a country. Language seemed to be hardly a barrier. A big grin and "Do you speak English?" was far more effective at getting people to talk than speaking broken Swedish. I never tire of congratulating Swedes on their high level of spoken English, which is a national triumph – and a rejoinder to countries such as France and Russia that believe some sort of language purity is necessary to safeguard the nation. I could follow the local papers thanks to Google Translate, which instantly produces a passable rendering of foreign news websites in English moments after the pages load.

However, my freelance gig for the *Guardian* suddenly dried up as the paper's finances took another dive. So why not write a book about Sweden's economy? On the other hand, as one of my Swedish friends put it: what on earth did I know about it? Fair point. I would find some people who did know about it, talk to them, and write down what they said. Bonnier, the publishing empire whose philanthropy has funded this book, is a big name in Sweden and would open doors, I surmised. Correctly, as it turned out. I have been granted privileged access to some of Sweden's top people.

I came to the subject as a blank slate, with very few preconceived notions and very little idea about what I would find. Most of the time I just tapped the recording icon on my phone and let people speak. Some of my most naive questions – "So is there a Swedish model then?" – turned out to be the most productive, either because people had different and conflicting answers, or because the issues were so simple and obvious that they had never thought about them properly before. In fact I think it may be one reason why this book has something interesting to say. This was a journey of discovery for me, and I am genuinely surprised, even excited, by what I found.

It is one of the conceits of my trade that journalists write about subjects with which they are only tenuously acquainted, using writerly tricks to make themselves seem authoritative nonetheless. I have done my best to become an authority, in the sense of reading everything I could find (mostly in English) about Sweden, and learning to read the papers in Swedish. Before I moved

13

here in 2013, I went to a big bookshop on Trafalgar Square in London to read up on my future home. I headed for the European History section, which was organised alphabetically by country name. There were lots of books on Spain, and a fair few on Turkey. But in between there was nothing at all about Scandinavia or Sweden.

This seemed odd because, in the UK at least, we have a minor love affair with the region. A TV mini-series in 2014 was even entitled "Scandimania", reflecting a fascination fuelled by the Nordic noir crime genre, the *Girl with the Dragon Tattoo* books and films, TV series such as *The Bridge* and *Wallander*, not to mention the huge popularity of Spotify, IKEA, H&M and other Swedish brands. Yet, with a few outstanding exceptions, most of the easily available books and documentaries about Scandinavia were little more than collections of lazy stereotypes. There seemed to be a need for something a more thoughtful about Sweden.

The empty hole on the bookshelf was partly, I would begin to suspect while doing my research, because many people interested in the idea of a "Swedish model" are on the political left, and the left decided 25 years ago that the Swedish model had failed. The main finding of this book is that it hasn't. But it has changed. On the political right, a generation ago the Swedish model seemed so closely associated with leftism that it made more sense to scrap all talk of a "model", rather than trying to reform it. Another finding of this book is that Sweden's reputation as a poster-child for the left is largely mistaken; many of the model's features appeal strongly to business, and the right has a case for reclaiming it as its own.

Discussions of Sweden tend to be over-politicised. One should bear in mind that for 13 of the past 27 years (this book is published in 2018), Sweden has been governed by parties of the centre right. Left and right should take credit – and share blame – for how the new Swedish model looks today. I hope the facts presented in this book will inspire, and provoke, people of widely different political persuasions.

The first three chapters are devoted to the internal workings of Sweden's economy: the role of the trade unions; the remarkable hidden welfare system that oils the economic wheels; and the unusual way in which Swedish capitalism is organised. The next three chapters look at more political aspects: the place of women and the family; the challenge of immigration and asylum; and the outlook of powerful figures on the left, right, and in business. Then we dive into the extraordinary story of Volvo Cars as an example of how the new Swedish model functions, and round off with a discussion of Sweden's ambitions to paint the model green.

Some of the topics covered here might seem at first glance to be a little dry. This is the fault of economists, who have given them a dry reputation. The extent to which this book manages to bring the issues to life will be a measure of its success.

To keep the text as readable as possible, I have not cluttered it with references. But at the end of the book you will find the sources of all the significant facts and quotes. I have tried to keep statistics – especially those dreadful "rankings" where Sweden always seems to come out on top – to a minimum, aiming instead to paint a broad picture on a large canvas.

Stockholm's waterfront. This book is a journey of discovery through Sweden's economy and society, starting from a blank slate with few preconceived notions about route or destination – apart perhaps from some of the usual stereotypes.

CHAPTER 1

WORKING LIFE:
'LESS BLOOD, SWEAT AND TEARS'

The unusual role of the trade unions in Sweden; why membership is still so high, even though the economy has done so well for so long; what business leaders have to say about the unions and how all this gave rise to a Swedish management style

It is all too easy to take a random personal experience and use it to make lazy generalisations that reinforce superficial notions about a foreign country. Like seeing a Frenchman carrying a string of onions. Or an American talking loudly. Or a Brit with bad teeth. I was reminded of this one pleasant June morning soon after I arrived in Gothenburg, when a garbage truck pulled up at the kerb in front of me. The door swung open and down stepped a willowy young blonde woman, her impossibly long, silky hair brushing against *lagom* sun-kissed skin. Wearing the grey overalls of the garbage company, she reached into the bin at the side of the road and slung its contents deftly into the back of the truck. I was dumbfounded. Try as I might, I could not avoid the fleeting thought that here was proof that everything I had ever heard about Sweden was true – a land of beautiful blondes and robust sexual equality.

But it doesn't take much digging to demonstrate that flaxen-haired sylphs are the exception among manual workers, rather than the rule. In fact, Sweden has a highly divided jobs market, with women concentrated in certain jobs. Rubbish collection is not one of them. As for the leggy blondeness, nobody has studied this with any degree of seriousness for a very long time.

I recommend simply walking through a crowded commuter train and trying to count the yellow-haired people – you won't see very many. Or visit a school and check out the kids. Karl Olov Arnstberg, an ethnologist who has studied "Swedishness" extensively, says the stereotype probably originates from a historical overgeneralisation about Sweden's mainly blonde movie stars. So my goddess in the garbage truck was almost entirely unrepresentative of both her profession, and her nation.

And yet, to British eyes, there is something different about Sweden, particularly when it concerns the world of work. At the airport in the capital, Stockholm, before I had immigrated full-time, I had some problems with my luggage. The woman who came to sort me out was also in overalls, but she looked me in the eye, spoke excellent English, and cut through my petty frustrations with a quiet confidence, a light touch and a certain pleasure in her work. This was far from the flustered ignorance, reluctance, or "not my problem" response I have come to expect in customer service situations elsewhere, especially in busy airports. And it is something I have encountered more than once in Sweden – people in jobs that might be considered "menial" in my home country behaving with poise, professionalism and pride. Shop assistants, waiters, ticket collectors, civil servants, electricians, bus drivers, gardeners – the sorts of ordinary people doing essential jobs with whom one interacts on a weekly basis – regularly demand respect, and give it back in return.

Hotel staff are likely to look bewildered if you offer them a tip for carrying your bags: they don't expect to tug their forelocks to earn their crust; there is usually a career structure in hotels, which is how staff aspire to advance at work through achieving the requisite training and qualifications. On restaurant bills, a service charge has not been itemised since the early 1990s, after unions signed an agreement with employers to regulate salaries across the industry. So your waiter is unlikely to be on a minimum wage, has probably undergone formal and sometimes prolonged training at a specialist vocational college, and has a sense of fulfilment and faith in the future. She doesn't necessarily want a tip, let alone expect it, because of the attendant implication that her living is dependent on your caprice and her deference, rather than on the right to receive a decent wage for performing a necessary service.

It is easy to put a rose-tinted gloss on all this, and I don't mean to exaggerate. But Sweden's egalitarian past and its surviving consensus approach to industrial relations have left subtle marks on society, most notably around the workplace. The unions are a force. While total membership has been drifting downwards, seven out of every 10 Swedish adults are members of a union – twice as many as in Italy, four times as many as in Germany, and almost 10 times more than France, the byword for industrial strife in Europe.

Employers who snub the unions can get into trouble. When swanky Stockholm restaurant Frantzén became the first in Sweden to be awarded a third Michelin star, early in 2018, the pubic celebrations were followed by uproar – it was revealed that Frantzén hadn't recognised the restaurant union. The irony was obvious. Here was an eatery owned by one of Sweden's richest woman, whose customers wouldn't bat an eyelid during a single visit to spend more than a week's wages for most workers, and yet the owners wouldn't play ball with the people who represent their chefs. It was shameful that Frantzén didn't want to take responsibility for its staff and for standards in the industry as a whole, the Hotel and Restaurants Union declared. "Other companies in the sector will think that if Frantzén lacks a collective agreement, they don't need one either. And then we will lose the entire Swedish model, and all the opportunities to develop the industry in a positive way," the union said.

More than 70 per cent of the hotel and restaurant industry is covered by union agreements. As if to prove its point, the union has produced a mobile phone app that enables you instantly to check which cafes and restaurants in Stockholm are unionised. As you wander through the city, Schysta Villkor – *Fair Conditions* – can help you choose somewhere to eat or drink at the same time as supporting "better conditions for workers". It is even a selling point for employers: being able to say "we have a collective agreement with the unions" may be attractive not just to customers at a cafe, but also to job seekers. Collective agreements regulate salaries but also a number of other conditions of employment, such as vacations, top-ups to the state's social insurance, severance periods and support during redundancy.

'CO-DECIDE WITH THE BOSS ON ALL KINDS OF SHIT'

This, then, is the first and the biggest of our Swedish bumblebees, which from a hard-nosed economic point of view perhaps ought not to fly. Nine out of 10 Swedish workers are employed in organisations where there are national agreements between the unions and management. In the public sector, it is 10 out of 10. For more than 40 years union leaders have sat on the boards of almost all companies with more than 25 workers, in most cases making up around a third of the board. Each year the unions and the employers' confederation negotiate private and public sector pay rises which apply across industry. And the employees themselves appear to be happy enough with all this, as we shall see later in this chapter. Although union membership has been declining, still around 70 per cent of all workers are members.

Trygghet för vanligt folk

Anders Malmström is one of them. Aged 41, he is an American working for Glue, a small tech startup in the capital. He has an MBA and an impeccable record in business management in the US and the UK. And he's a union member. He had never joined a union before, but when he went to work for a startup it made sense for him to be part of a union, because of the safety net it offers, but also the advice and support, personally and as an employer – many small startups are often lacking in the Human Resources area. "For me, unions are something associated with big, old, traditional companies," he says. "But they are the ones that need it least, both because they have the most job security. Here things can change quickly."

Malmström is a member of Civilekonomerna, the Swedish Association of Graduates in Business Administration and Economics. He pays about €40 ($50) a month for his union membership and unemployment insurance, which will cover 80 per cent of his salary up to a pretty high ceiling "if it all goes south". The safety net works for Sweden in terms of entrepreneurship, says this father of three, because it gives people a platform to take risks. "Unions to me are a relic of the past, so it is cool for me to see how they have transformed into something living with the times," he says.

Relics of the past are exactly the things that strike you when you walk into the Stockholm headquarters of LO, the huge Trade Union Confederation that organises 1.5 million blue-collar workers, or a third of Sweden's workforce. In the small park opposite, there stands a 1950s bronze relief of the founder of Swedish social democracy, Hjalmar Branting, towering over his devoted followers and looking disturbingly like Joseph Stalin. Once inside the building, you are greeted by a similarly over-proportioned figure – a heroic, Aryan worker, his chiseled torso worthy of a men's fitness magazine, holding a large pair of tongs that grasp an ingot of red-hot metal.

The fresco by Olle Hjortzberg, who seems to have taken time out here from his usual religious imagery – unless you worship the male physique, that is – dates from the late 1930s, shortly after the unions acquired the building. This was the decade when a cornerstone was laid beneath Sweden's economic model. A landmark agreement with the employers, named after the Saltsjöbaden hotel in Stockholm where it was negotiated, launched an era of consensus and collaboration between capital and labour. The Saltsjöbaden agreement, signed on December 20 1938, provides the basis for Sweden's consensus-driven approach to labour relations and is the "bedrock" of the Swedish model of capitalism, according to the Financial Times. Even today,

< The offices of LO, the blue-collar trade union confederation.
  The banner reads: Security for ordinary people.

"WE LET THE EMPLOYERS KNOW WE HAVE THE RIGHT TO STRIKE, BUT THAT RIGHT IS MOST EFFECTIVE WHEN YOU DON'T ACTUALLY NEED TO USE IT."

Karl-Petter Thorwaldsson, *the boss of blue-collar workers union LO*

80 years on, Sweden is characterised by relative industrial peace and an extremely low level of strikes.

Karl-Petter Thorwaldsson, the boss of LO, looks like he has not had a chiseled torso for some time. But despite some middle-aged spread, the youthful-looking 53-year-old bounces with energy, rattling off the positive features of an economic model based on high trade union membership. Since 1997, the wages of the average LO member have gone up an astonishing 60 per cent in real terms, he says, thanks to low inflation and high productivity growth. "That must be a world record!" Thorwaldsson says. The trade union ethic has deep roots in Swedish society, he explains:

"Most employers gain more by being inside the system than out ... It gives us an advantage over other countries. If you want to make an investment, the first thing you look at is competitiveness, and whether the workers expect and favour change. Swedish workers are well known for their pragmatism. The second thing you look at is the number of strike days – our model has one of the lowest levels of strikes in the world. The employers know we have the right to strike, but that right is most effective when you don't actually need to use it."

Wages in Sweden have indeed shot up in the past two decades, according to the OECD, far more than anywhere in northern Europe except for oil-

rich Norway. This good outcome for Swedish workers is an enviable consequence of strong economic growth that in turn is a result of decades of stable relations between management and unions.

In Britain, as I know from personal experience as a union organiser at the *Financial Times*, workers tend to join unions as an insurance policy against bad times, rather than because things are going well at work. A short stroll from LO's imposing headquarters is a building that is home to another story altogether. This mundane office bloc is mission control for TCO, the white-collar union federation, whose recent history suggests unions can be essential to a modern workforce, even during the good times. The federation has attracted a remarkable 400,000 new members in the past 10 years – an increase of 40 per cent. As a result, TCO is snapping at the heels of its blue collar rival, and soon expects to become Sweden's biggest union federation. It boasts 74 per cent membership across white collar sectors.

The unions that make up TCO have been so successful partly because Sweden's workforce is changing, but also because they changed their approach a decade ago after a membership slump. "We realised that even though trade unions were very much needed, young people could not identify with the image we portrayed – they would picture a grey-haired man with a flag in his hand demonstrating on the streets," says Eva Nordmark, head of TCO. The union's members generally have a good working life and good job security. They like their jobs and are doing well, but want to do better. So after much thought, the federation changed not what it does, but how it communicates about it, Nordmark says:

"If we as unions only talk about what's wrong and how bad everything is, workers don't recognise it. You cannot just describe working life as bad – you have to see the potential and possibilities, people want to be happy."

Marina Åman, head of Unionen, the largest union inside the TCO federation, describes how her union intoned the trinity of framgång, trygghet och glädje i arbetslivet – success, security and happiness at work. "We want to make our members feel good about going to work, it would be devastating if they didn't enjoy it," she says. The white-collar unions also embraced economic change. Sweden is a better, wealthier country today because the unions are open to structural change, Åman says. "We tend to see change as something positive

27

< The Stockholm headquarters of TCO, the white-collar trade union confederation.

"IF WE AS UNIONS ONLY TALK ABOUT WHAT'S WRONG AND HOW BAD EVERYTHING IS, WORKERS DON'T RECOGNISE IT. YOU CANNOT JUST DESCRIBE WORKING LIFE AS BAD — YOU HAVE TO SEE THE POTENTIAL AND POSSIBILITIES, PEOPLE WANT TO BE HAPPY."

Eva Nordmark, *head of TCO*

28

because it drives evolution forward — but we need to take into account the consequences for the individual."

This is what makes Swedish trade unions different — they don't just say no to everything. They also say yes to free trade, yes to globalisation, yes to digitalisation, yes even to transatlantic trade deals, opposed by unions elsewhere who fear opening up their domestic markets to greater foreign competition. One of the reasons for this attitude to change is Sweden's unique system for helping workers into new jobs, which we will explore in Chapter 3. "We are not afraid of structural change because we have this safety system for our members," Nordmark says:

"Our view has never been to protect jobs, but to protect our members. Our focus is on your next job. You don't want to get stuck in a bad job that you don't like or that you're not good at. Productivity is very important to us because we want Sweden to be a wealthy country. So the unions have not protected old, bad jobs — instead we protect our members. We want them to have new, better jobs. It is important that companies are successful, because that is where our members' salaries come from."

To get a flavour of the kind of trade unionism espoused by Nordmark and Åman, let's look at the series of viral videos in English, French and German that TCO has produced in recent years. Using the hash tag #likeaswede, they set

out to sell the Swedish model abroad. The tongue-in-cheek videos introduced a character, "Joe Williams", a US citizen who could afford to live "like a Swede", with holidays, parental leave, a decent pension and so on. The idea was to show how people in unionised workplaces in Sweden can enjoy the benefits usually available only to the rich in other countries. Recorded in Los Angeles, the video went viral in North America, becoming the second most shared video on YouTube in its first 24 hours and generating some popular memes. Another TCO video, "Business like a Swede", is set to music, with performers who rap:

[employer] I treat my employees with love and respect
We have a collective agreement no one can reject
We agree on great perks, talk straight and direct
And the rising pile of money means it's having effect
[employee] We get parental leave, plus the six weeks vay-cay
So that when we get back to work we're on our A-game
Co-decide with the boss on all kinds of shit
And the company fitness programme keeps us lookin' fit
We be like bread and butter, we be like wine and cheese
With the collective agreement for industrial peace
Business like a Swede, two parts in decision-making
Business like a Swede, it's a win-win situation

'PEOPLE WHO WANT TO BE INVOLVED'

Let's accept that the collective power of the unions has underpinned relatively high average wages for workers. But how does management see things? In 2017, an expert body set up by Swedish employers surveyed attitudes towards the unions among chief executives. CEOs were positive about the benefits of talking to the unions, particularly the reputation it gave them with their employees. A collective agreement also improved relations with employees and made it easier to set salary levels, they said. They were neutral on whether dealing with the unions reduced their flexibility or entailed higher wages.

Company bosses were also asked if they would maintain agreements in place even if the unions' right to strike were scrapped. A clear majority – 61 per cent – said they would still like to have agreements, while only 15 per cent said no. The result suggests an overwhelmingly positive attitude towards the unions, particularly among big companies. Eight out of 10 CEOs of companies with more than 250 employees said they would hold onto union agreements regardless.

But what about other aspects of the model, such as workers having a voice on company boards? The very thought would cause sleepless nights for bosses in the United States or Britain. Carl-Peter Forster, a senior German businessman, is well placed to judge. Forster had a career spanning big-name German, US, British and Indian car companies before he joined the board of Volvo Cars in Gothenburg in 2013. For five years he was also chairman of Saab, the Swedish carmaker, before it was devastated by the slump that followed the 2008 global financial crisis.

"I am German, so I think I can talk a little about labour and the unions," he says in a spacious office in Lindholmen, the gleaming, high-tech science park that has replaced the docks in the centre of Gothenburg. Swedish labour relations are not the same as the system in Germany, which also allows worker representatives onto company boards, Forster says. German company boards are typically 50:50 workers and management, which can create an impasse that leads to a difficult process of finding a compromise position on which both sides can agree. In Sweden, however, while the unions are participate at board level, it seems they are neither legally nor formally as strong as in Germany:

31

"Sweden has found an interesting model of labour participation, which I am a believer in. Labour representatives understand business, the challenges and what makes business successful. So as far as they are participating in that discussion, it makes things inherently better for everybody, and ultimately better for society. In this sense the Swedish model is clearly an interesting alternative to the German system."

The labour participation model in Sweden, combined with a culture of consensus, has created a stable business environment that is "more flexible" than the German system, Forster continues. The unions enjoy a good position in the system, but they still allow industry to come to decisions more easily and with a smaller degree of formal compromise than in Germany. The culture is "massively consensual" while allowing people to have robustly different opinions. This is combined with "an almost complete lack of hierarchy":

"This is quite amazing, I have never seen a country that is less hierarchical, it is more egalitarian than any other. ... You have very informed labour representatives, which you do not have in Britain and you absolutely don't have in the US. Also you avoid the pitfalls of France and Spain, where unions are outside management and very combative, very confrontational and left wing, and do not understand the challenges of industry and business."

At the highest levels of Swedish management there appears to be an almost embarrassed acceptance of the system of strong unions. Industry in the 1970s used to be very sceptical of having unions on company boards, says Leif Johansson, former Volvo CEO and now chairman of the Anglo-Swedish pharmaceutical powerhouse AstraZeneca. Johansson says:

"My father thought it would not go well – but in fact it has worked. If you sit around the table for 20 years, over time you get a shared understanding of what needs to be done, often the unions don't trust a single thing that management says. The Swedish unions have become part of the entrepreneurial business model. You build consensus around the table, which makes strikes and lockouts a last resort rather than first resort. It has made it difficult for aggressive employers or unions to do something dramatically different from everyone else."

Peter Zhang, a Chinese executive who played a key role in Geely's acquisition of Volvo Cars in 2010 (see Chapter 7), and who until 2018 sat on Volvo's board, says he was warned before he came to Sweden about the high wages and strong unions, which he refers to as "Swedish socialism". But now he is reconciled to them:

"Socialistic aspects of Sweden include the consultation culture, which is quite unique. It is something I started to learn about when I spent more time here and became part of the board. People are more used to talking about things and to trying to find a common forum before they commit themselves to actions. People might argue this hinders efficiency, but once the decision has been made after this consultation process, once people feel part of it, they have a sense of ownership, which is good."

Ronnie Leten, Belgian chairman of Ericsson and former CEO of Swedish mining company Atlas Copco, says the unions have a very good sense of the feeling among workers on the ground, "better even than the CEO and managers sometimes", and they bring this insight to company boards:

"Having worked in many countries, I think this is a good model. It has not held us back at Atlas or Electrolux in taking decisions. For me this is the modern way of working. In the companies I lead everyone has degrees, they read newspapers, they are educated, so it's not a matter of me knowing better. You have to work in participation, people want to be part of it

and understand why – when they understand, then they work together with you. You can call it unions, or you can call it people who want to be involved."

Several senior executives said the unions actually made it easier to sack people, rather than more complicated. If Annika or Sven doesn't fit with your company, you can negotiate with a sensible union representative, not with the workers directly – which makes life easier for management. "The unions are very reasonable, they are on the company's side," said Jane Walerud, a successful investor behind companies such as Klarna, which enables online purchases where you pay after you get the goods. If someone isn't working well, the unions know about it before management, she said. Hans Enocson, outgoing boss of GE in Sweden, made a similar point:

"It is easier here than in many countries to trim the tree. French and German unions are much more difficult to deal with."

The unions are particularly useful when it comes to tough decisions like closing a factory, said Håkan Mogren, board member of the Investor group owned by the powerful Wallenberg family. By informing them from the beginning, you can convince them that closing the factory is good for the company as a whole, Mogren said: "And the unions buy that argument. From this specific point of view it gives Sweden a competitive advantage." Indeed, unions sometimes fear that legal requirements of confidentiality mean they are trapped, party to business secrets that they cannot immediately share with the workforce and obliged to take part in painful decisions that they must later defend.

Not everyone is convinced. Consensus can be slow, and at the end of the day, employment rights have to be respected, which ties the hands of management. Keith McLoughlin, from 2011 to 2016 the American CEO of Swedish domestic appliance manufacturer Electrolux, says he found it "a little bit shocking at first" when he realised union members sat on company boards in Sweden. As a more consensus driven culture, things take longer here, he says; they are a little slower. In the US, the CEO debates with his team then says: "Here's what we are going to do," so everyone runs out and does it. But in Sweden, the response is: "Well, thanks for that input," McLoughlin says. He found he had to adjust and learn to convince people one-on-one. But the system works "fundamentally", he says, because union members start with an assumption that the company's success is in their own best interest:

"When I became CEO I realised that the nature of the relationship between unions and company leaders is quite different. They start with the premise that says: 'We understand that the company has to make money and provide value for shareholders.' My experience of unions in the US is that they say to management: 'That's your problem, that's what you get paid to deal with, while our issue is to maximise the benefit to our members.' In Sweden at least, unions and management start on the same page. Of course there are disagreements, but the unions come at it from a perspective of asking: 'Is this the correct long-term perspective?' It's a different mindset. You can get a lot more done with a lot less blood, sweat and tears."

'1,000 PEOPLE TAKING INITIATIVES'

As education levels rise and more organisations seek to make use of their employees' intellectual capital, steep hierarchies seem to be losing their appeal in many countries. But it is one thing to regard hierarchies as less influential than before – it is quite another to attach an negative value to hierarchical structures, as some Swedish companies have done to great effect. Facing strong unions, a tradition of consensus and a broader culture of egalitarianism, some have made a virtue out of a necessity. Management methods have emerged from Sweden's unusual workplace milieu that may be well suited to modern, complex organisations in which skilled workers produce innovative and sophisticated products and services.

Much academic ink has been spilled trying to establish the existence of a particular Swedish leadership style. According to this work, distinguishing characteristics of Swedish management include a preference for teamwork and co-operation, a non-hierarchical approach, emphasis on consensus and conflict-avoidance, encouragement of autonomy and delegation of authority. A typical Swedish management instruction might therefore be: "See what you can do about it," rather than issuing direct orders. A book of interviews with Swedish managers in 2008 concluded that their leadership style should be seen as a product of the country's egalitarian society, and was likely to be successful in the current era:

"A flat corporate structure is a logical and cost-efficient way to operate, innovate and recruit."

No other company has made more of its Swedish management culture than IKEA – there is much more to Swedishness at an IKEA store than its minimalist products, blue-and-yellow façade and meatballs on the menu. At the heart of "the IKEA way", the management philosophy exported to Europe in the 1980s, is a powerful notion that the company is run according to Swedish principles. Managers would be whisked away to the corporate headquarters in Älmhult, the small town in the depths of the Småland countryside where the late Ingvar Kamprad founded his empire, to help them absorb the local way of doing things.

Managers were encouraged to learn Swedish if they wanted to make a successful career, according to Anders Moberg, Kamprad's CEO for 15 years. They would be expected to move to Sweden for a while, living and working in the Swedish environment. "When we had infused them with the Swedish way, after two or three years we would send them back home and they would be better than the Swedes!" Moberg says. "They were our future leaders."

Some aspects of this management style were more obvious than others. Informality was in, so ties were out, says Johan Stenebo, formerly one of Kamprad's most trusted lieutenants and author of a tell-all book about the company. Today it seems like a minor thing, but abandoning ties sent a powerful signal about the company's values. "In those days it was trail-blazing," Stenebo says. Similarly, after Sweden in the late 1960s moved to ditch the formal second person plural in favour of the singular pronoun *du*, IKEA did the same in Germany, branding the shift as the Swedish way. It also did away with titles, so managers and workers referred to each other on a first name basis. Moberg says:

"People said we were crazy. But it created a very good atmosphere, less distance between management and the people working for us ... People really liked to work in an environment like that, where it was not hierarchical and you could talk to the boss as he was on the shop floor. We had a flat organisation, not many levels. You could go to the boss if there was something you didn't like – relations with the staff were very straightforward. Many young people grew up with IKEA and spent the rest of their life with us, they felt at home. Lots of people don't feel comfortable in the hierarchical way of being managed, where the boss is God."

Kamprad himself summed it up in the penultimate paragraph of his *Testament of a Furniture Dealer*, written in 1976, which became a bible for IKEA managers:

"MANY YOUNG PEOPLE GREW UP WITH IKEA AND SPENT THE REST OF THEIR LIFE WITH US, THEY FELT AT HOME. LOTS OF PEOPLE DON'T FEEL COMFORTABLE IN THE HIERARCHICAL WAY OF BEING MANAGED, WHERE THE BOSS IS GOD"

Anders Moberg, *IKEA's CEO for 15 years*

36

"Humbleness is the key word. Being humble means so much to us in our work and in our leisure. It is even decisive for us as human beings. It means not just consideration and respect for our fellow men and women, but also kindness and generosity. Will-power and strength without humbleness often lead to conflict. Together with humbleness, will-power and strength are your secret weapons for development as an individual and fellow human being."

IKEA was 40 years ahead of Silicon Valley in this respect, Stenebo says – working for the company was like being at Google or Facebook today. The attractiveness for Brits or Germans was that Swedishness was something exotic, everyone was on first name terms and there were lots of symbols of working as a group. "People bought into it 100 per cent and felt proud," he says.

Stenebo is sceptical that IKEA still embodies this approach today. His book, while in many ways a panegyric to Kamprad, also set out to demolish the idealised image of egalitarianism at IKEA. In reality, Stenebo claimed, it was a secretive dictatorship run with an iron fist by the Kamprad family with help from a network of internal "spies" who reported on any senior managers displaying signs of disloyalty. Moberg is more positive: the IKEA way is still very much alive, he says.

Who is right? Here is what American Ginny Figlar, who recently spent five years at IKEA HQ in Älmhult as a copywriter, concluded after her Swedish experience:

"At work, people felt more like family than co-workers (and still do). There were no egos. There was no hierarchy. This made working in a corporate environment quite refreshing, but it also meant that decisions were made by committee. In other words, they weren't made very quickly. But everyone worked together, respected each other and had fun. Despite the hard work, people came first. Life came first. You could say the stuff that matters most came first. I've often reflected on my time working there and wondered if what I experienced was because I was living in Sweden or working at IKEA. The line always seemed blurred to me. Was it the Swedish culture or the IKEA culture?"

Are IKEA's management methods more widely applied in Swedish business? Tobii is a Swedish high-tech company that develops products for tracking the movement of people's eyes. Walking into the company's offices in Danderyd, Stockholm, feels more like entering a university department than the headquarters of a multinational corporation. From behind his large and messy desk, Henrik Eskilsson, founder and CEO, is eloquent about his leadership philosophy:

"A very hierarchical, top-down structure is effective in organising an army, where one person tells 1,000 people what to do. In a modern economy, the winning system is most likely to be the one that enables 1,000 people in a company to collaborate effectively – without one person telling the other 999 what to do, but rather 1,000 taking initiatives, having ideas, being proactive. You need 1,000 people doing the creative thinking, coming up with innovative ideas. The Swedish culture is well adapted to that, to dare to take decisions and make stuff happen."

Eskilsson complains that he is treated differently in the US, where employees expect him to be obeyed. When he whispers at the company's Silicon Valley offices, people jump. The Swedish leadership style confuses North Americans – they think it's relaxing, nobody is screaming at them so they can lean back and take it easy. As a result, Tobii has to retrain them, Eskilsson says. In Sweden, however, people are already accustomed to being autonomous and to taking decisions themselves. The hierarchy is there, just not so important: "We shouldn't let an option win just because it comes from the manager."

The flat society in Sweden means top management is approachable and receptive, according to Lex Kerssemakers, the Dutch boss of Volvo Cars in the US. "Some people think it is anarchy," he says, and sometimes it is – but good ideas can flourish and are not always stopped by middle layers. "People here are raised to believe that everyone is equal and has the same rights, so they feel they can speak up, they are not hindered by feeling that they can't talk to that person because he is a few levels up," Kerssemakers says. "You see that with graduates here, they are very open, sometimes even a little naive, they just talk to you. That means they have been raised in an open environment."

The Swedish tendency to question authority is perfect for complex software development teams, according to Stina Ehrensvärd, CEO and founder of Yubico, a developer of IT security technology. Ehrensvärd moved from Sweden to California in 2011 to build her company. But in the US, her Swedish approach can create confusion, she says:

"Sweden has the flattest organisations in the world, it's okay to question your boss. Nobody can know everything, so I am super open, I am constantly telling my team they know more than me in their expert areas. In the US people can be confused by this approach. The Swedes question me much more. In the US they are starting to do so, because now they know I'm not going to fire them for it. In countries where you are constantly punished for questioning and doing things that parents, teachers, the state, the emperor says you can't do, people get afraid, they don't want to speak up."

39

My own experience of working life in Sweden is limited, but still I have something to add. For two years I have worked part-time as the editor of a company intranet, the internal website, for a mid-sized company (ie multinational company) making complex security equipment. My manager has been exceptionally trusting and flexible. In essence, her approach has been: "I don't mind where or when you do it, just get the job done on time to a high standard and I will be happy – but always tell me when you screw up." She knows I have a certain set of skills, and I am clear about my work goals, so she doesn't need to micro-manage me. However, whenever my concentration slips, or big life events get in the way (like writing a book), she steps in to steady the ship. This approach applies to the whole marketing and communications team, and it works very well. Since I joined the company she has been promoted to the Group Executive Team. I am sure the two things could not be a co-incidence.

SUMMARY CHAPTER 1

Summing up, what have we learned about the Swedish bumblebee?

• For every Swede that fits your stereotype of the nation, I can show you 10 who don't.

• The trade unions in Sweden are broadly attractive to large numbers of the population, regardless of their profession.

• The unions' approach is to look after their members, rather than particular jobs, so they largely embrace the logic of globalisation and the frequent economic upheaval it entails.

• Most employers actively want to negotiate with the trade unions – they are not forced to do so.

• This approach helps to maintain industrial peace, with a very low level of strikes

• This system has created a Swedish management style characterised by consensus and a relatively flat hierarchy.

• In a nutshell, it means managers can manage with a lot less blood, sweat and tears.

CHAPTER 2

BETWEEN JOBS: SWEDEN'S HIDDEN WELFARE SYSTEM

One woman's unemployment crisis; why employers and unions set wages centrally and help people change jobs; how the system rose, died, and rose again; how tough love lubricates the labour market; some additional benefits

For Gunilla Stensson, life was looking good. She had a steady job as a web developer, living with her daughter in a picturesque village in Bohuslän, the stunning wilderness on Sweden's west coast. Gothenburg was a simple train ride away. A short walk from home was a sandy beach belonging to one of the thousands of lakes that scatter Sweden's glacial landscape. In 20 minutes by car she could be island-hopping on the stunning archipelago, where the coast slowly dissolves into the clear, dark waters of the Kattegat.

But then, a new boss at Stensson's work demanded change, and the office was moved to Stockholm. For Gunilla, with her daughter at a local school and her life so settled, that meant only one thing – she was out of a job.

At first, things seemed rosy. Stensson became self-employed and began dreaming of an independent life with her own business. But then the bad luck started. A job offer from a nearby college seemed less risky and stressful. It turned out to be the opposite – the following year she suffered a breakdown. She tried to ease herself back into work with part-time study, but a student grant quickly ran out. Dozens of job applications ended in rejection. And on top of all that, her former husband was no longer sharing their daughter's upbringing.

Four years into her crisis, Stensson found herself alone, aged 47, with no business, no job, no money, and no self-confidence. A support group with other unemployed people only reinforced the doubts she had about herself, namely that she was a single mother living in the sticks who had been out of work for a long time.

"I was really down," she says. "I can understand people who think about suicide when they lose their job." She toyed with trying to start her own business again, but soon realised this was not the right time in her life. But there were so many people looking for jobs in her line of work, and her confidence was low. She felt she hadn't had proper employment for almost five years, and her skills were out of date. But Svensson had a lifeline.

Her original employer subscribed to *Trygghetsrådet*, or TRR, which loosely translates as the Security Council. This is a partnership between employers and the unions that provides expert support to redundant workers. The agency commits to work for five years with a person to get them back on track. Stensson turned to them and was assigned a counsellor, whom she met every couple of weeks. TRR also paid for a course of psychotherapy. She says:

44

"I felt all the time that they believed in me, that was the key point. I felt I was worthless, I was not getting any interviews. But they didn't look at that part of me, only at that part of me that does have knowledge and skills. As soon as I took the decision that I didn't want my own business but I wanted a job, they started guiding me in that direction, but not in an aggressive way – it was as if they knew where I was and could support me at each point. Their approach was to actually get this person going again, not just to get rid of them as fast as possible."

When at last Stensson was invited to an interview, TRR arranged coaching over Skype while she was out of town. Her sister-in-law took her to buy a new outfit, and she nailed the job.

Barely a year later, Stensson flashes a confident smile over lunch in Gothenburg, where she is taking a break from her new job. She looks every bit the sassy internet professional that has just secured employment in the healthcare system – she is calm and engaged, able to talk openly about her recent problems without embarrassment or self-pity. "It felt so easy after I went to TRR," Stensson giggles. "There was a shift inside me, I found my confidence again – that was the big thing I got from TRR. I don't know what would have happened without them. It was so important to have someone who kept believing in me."

**"THERE WAS A SHIFT INSIDE ME, I FOUND MY CONFIDENCE AGAIN
– THAT WAS THE BIG THING I GOT FROM TRR. I DON'T KNOW WHAT
WOULD HAVE HAPPENED WITHOUT THEM. IT WAS SO IMPORTANT
TO HAVE SOMEONE WHO KEPT BELIEVING IN ME."**

Gunilla Stensson, *web developer*

Stensson's story is just one among those of the many thousands of Swedish workers who find themselves out of a job each year, and who make their way to a job security agency such as TRR. When we think about Sweden's famously generous welfare state, we tend to think about tax-payer funded benefits, including those for the unemployed. But job security agencies – *trygghetsfonder* in Swedish, known collectively as the transition system, or *omställningssystem* – are a unique and largely hidden aspect of the county's welfare setup, funded entirely by employers. TRR, one of the largest, is backed by about 35,000 private sector companies with nearly one million employees, almost a quarter of the workforce.

Companies typically pay 0.3 per cent of their wage bill each year into the security agencies, of which there are 10. In good years for the economy, when layoffs are low, money swells the agencies' coffers as insurance against the bad times. On average, TRR spends around €2,600 on each person who turns to it for help, but that average conceals wide variations – the agency places no limits on the amount it will spend on training, coaching and counselling to get someone back into work. It also tops up the unemployment benefit paid out by the state and trade union unemployment insurance schemes. "Our goal," TRR says, "is to try and make sure the time from one job to another should be as short, effective and as meaningful as possible."

Welfare is too often associated with handouts. In Sweden, looking after people during difficult times is a long way from this. The country's transition

"I FELT ALL THE TIME THAT THEY BELIEVED IN ME, THAT WAS THE KEY POINT. I FELT I WAS WORTHLESS, I WAS NOT GETTING ANY INTERVIEWS, MY BUSINESS HADN'T GOT STARTED. BUT THEY DIDN'T LOOK AT THAT PART OF ME, ONLY AT THAT PART OF ME THAT DOES HAVE KNOWLEDGE AND SKILLS. THEY REFLECTED THIS BACK AT ME."

Gunilla Stensson

46

system, with the job security agencies at its heart, is an important part of explaining how Sweden's economy maintains its global competitiveness, despite such an apparently well paid workforce. Helping the unemployed back into work, enabling them to improve their skills or recover from the stresses of redundancy, and making sure they are not penniless during the process, has a strict economic rationale.

To understand how this unique system – a sort of private welfare state within the welfare state – has come about, we must look briefly at the origins of Sweden's unusual labour market, where the focus is on protecting the individual worker, rather than protecting his or her job. This is a story of the rise, fall, and improbable rise again of a unique feature of the way Sweden does business. If ever a bumblebee shouldn't fly, it is this one.

WHY SWEDISH WORKERS LOVE THE MARKET

Behind the scenes, two Swedes helped to shape the country's economy during the post-War decades. In the early 1950s, Gösta Rehn and Rudolf Meidner were researchers at LO, the blue-collar union federation. They had learned their craft in Stockholm as pupils of Gunnar Myrdal, who went on to win a Nobel Prize for economics. Both were members of the Social Democratic Party, Rehn on the right – he volunteered to fight the Soviets when they invaded Finland in 1939 – and Meidner somewhere in the main-

stream of a party that had long since rejected talk of social revolution. Meidner came from a German Jewish family that had fled the Nazis in 1933; later, his radical ideas about evolutionary roads to socialism would place him on the far left of the Social Democrats. Neither man was a self-publicist, preferring to address questions of practical economics in trade union and party newspapers, rather than producing books like the one you are currently holding.

The problem Rehn and Meidner tackled was this: how, with labour in short supply, could Sweden's rapidly expanding economy continue to grow without generating an upward spiral of wages and inflation? In 1951, at LO's national congress, they presented their solution, now known – mostly to a narrow circle of economists – as the Rehn-Meidner model.

In a traditional market for labour, employers compete with each other to hire workers, driving up wages in those sectors where profitability, and therefore the ability to pay those wages, is higher. This creates pockets of high and low pay across the economy, and sows strife within the unions as members in one sector see their wages rise while others lag behind. To prevent this from happening, Rehn and Meidner made the following proposal: wages should be set centrally, on the principle that workers doing broadly similar jobs should get roughly the same wages – regardless of a company's ability to pay them.

Such a system automatically favours profitable firms, for which the centrally determined wages are affordable, meaning they can invest their profits into further expansion instead of having to fight off wage demands from workers wanting a bigger slice of the pie. Simultaneously, companies – even entire sectors – with low profitability are forced either to raise their game to pay higher wages, or to shut down altogether.

The system is deliberately designed to secure a shift in employment from lower to higher productivity enterprises. In this way, Rehn and Meidner argued, the overall productivity of Swedish industry would be boosted, as non-productive industry would have to adapt or die. Companies with low productivity would be denied the life-line of cutting wages to survive. Moreover, if wage levels were set by those sectors that are competing on world markets, productivity would be driven by global manufacturing standards, ensuring that Swedish companies stayed internationally competitive. At the same time, competitive businesses would generate tax revenues to continue funding a generous welfare state.

Sweden's employers were receptive to this idea. Collective agreements and central coordination of pay increases, they reasoned, would dampen wage pressures arising from competition for workers and local trade union militancy. The country's export-oriented corporations already faced fierce competition from their global counterparts, so they had to keep their wage costs below the level dictated by the domestic market. To be able to do this, they needed to control the process of wage formation. Since their famous truce of 1938, union and business leaders had established a degree of mutual trust, which would be essential for a wages system such as that proposed by Rehn and Meidner. Even more attractive to business was that unions would agree not to launch any strikes once pay negotiations were concluded, which meant industrial peace was hard-wired into the model.

Workers, however, would need to accept losing their jobs as global market forces drove Swedish industry to constantly restructure itself. To sugar this pill, the Social Democratic government agreed to generous unemployment bene-fits and "active" labour market policies, helping workers between jobs to retrain and re-skill themselves to enter expanding, profitable sectors. The traditional trade union demand for job security was replaced by *security of transition* into new jobs. The system therefore encouraged rationalisation and efficiency, but demanded public investment in education and training in return.

This unusual aspect of the Swedish model is almost tailor-made to accom-modate the "creative destruction" that liberal economists describe as the fun-damental dynamic of capitalism, says Thomas Carlén, a descendant of Rehn and Meidner at the economics research department of LO. "Because the Nor-dic model is focused on managing labour transitions," he says, "security lies in the notion of employability, rather than in the protection of existing jobs. The model is designed to facilitate restructuring. The state, unions and employ-ers ensure that there are measures available to support displaced workers in finding new jobs."

This Swedish adaptation of Keynesian economics was a distinctly liberal, pro-market solution. As Meidner himself put it many years later:

"[Swedish] Labour market policy was to be used as a means to remove hindrances for a market economy of the type that the classical economic theorists dreamed of. The element of planning in this quasi-liberal ideology was reduced to the method for eliminating these hindrances. When the economy was freed from this, it was thought that it could function accord-ing to the rules of the market, and so do even better than in a consistently non-interventionist society."

Some unusual consequences followed from this. First, the Swedish trade unions became pro-market and pro-globalisation. They saw the value of milk-ing the capitalist cow rather than trying to slaughter it, but decided that they

Johan Sandgren, advisor for TRR, a partnership between employers and trade unions to provide expert support to unemployed workers: "Our goal is to make sure the time from one job to another is as short and as meaningful as possible."

had to keep it healthy to get the most milk. Consequently there were many examples in the 1960s of union representatives at both national and local level agreeing to job losses in stagnating, low-wage industries such as textiles, where they would refer to the need for a mobile workforce and structural change. To this day, LO says it regards globalisation, structural transformation, technical advances and openness to the world as "opportunities rather than threats", and it backs free trade instead of protectionism.

This attitude has taken root in Swedish society. In an official EU survey in 2017, 86 per cent of Swedes – the highest among all EU countries – agreed with the statement that "globalisation is an opportunity for economic growth", compared to an EU average of 62 per cent. The Rehn-Meidner framework also created a powerful moral climate that discouraged workers from sitting back and enjoying their unemployment benefits. Payment of compensation was often conditional on accepting job offers or re-training schemes, and it came to be seen as verging on the criminal not to relocate and take jobs in other cities.

There was a ruthless pragmatism behind the encouragement of the workforce to move to where it was needed. Says Johannes Lindvall, professor of political science at Lund University:

"There was a lot of pressure on the unemployed precisely because we had these training programmes, which essentially forced people to move to other cities to get work. It is a mistake to think that the model was a cushy, collectivist system that emphasised only rights and not responsibilities – but there was also a lot of investment when people made the transition to new jobs."

The system of centralised wage bargaining also gave rise to a remarkably flat society in terms of earned income, with minimal differentials between workers' wages. Wages for the lowest paid were – and still are – higher than the salary that the market wants to pay, while wages for higher paid workers were similarly lower than a level set by a free market in labour. For this reason this was known as a policy of "solidarity wages". From the early 1960s to the early 1980s, the wage distribution for blue-collar workers was compressed by a whopping 75 per cent, so that a pay rise of 30 per cent was enough to carry a worker from the lowest 10 per cent all the way to the highest.

In a more conventional labour market, this might be seen as destroying incentives for workers to improve their productivity – how can managers encourage their staff without the carrot of financial reward? In sharp contrast with the United States, Sweden showed a weak relation between the value added per worker – their productivity – and their wages. Nevertheless, this unusual set-up seems to have delivered a sharp boost to Sweden's overall economy, at least in the early stages. Pushing workers into productive parts of industry raised productivity by around eight percentage points, and output by 20 percentage points.

HUMPTY DUMPTY – SWEDISH VERSION

The Rehn-Meidner model worked well in an economy where many workers were doing similar tasks, which could be measured so their work could be compared. But gradually, under political and economic pressures, the system began to creak at the seams. Several factors were at work. The unions were being pulled in different directions. Workers in profitable sectors demanded higher wages, while the left sought to flatten incomes even further by boosting the wages of the lower paid, regardless of what work they did. In the winter of 1969, thousands of miners launched a two-month wildcat strike in the far north, demanding better wages and conditions, which encouraged further strikes elsewhere.

53

When Swedish industry was hit by the global slowdown in the mid-1970s, divisions arose between employers. Some began to seek a transition away from mass production methods towards more flexibility, entailing the dissolution of central wage bargaining; others preferred to hold down wages through the central bargaining framework. Throughout the 1970s inflation grew, and wage rises galloped to keep up. Rising costs forced Swedish governments to devalue the currency repeatedly to save the country's international competitiveness, further fuelling inflation and wage hikes.

Meanwhile, a proposal gained momentum that companies should place a portion of their shares under the unions' control, which would increase over time. Employers were furious – these "wage-earner funds" were seen by business as a dangerous attack on private ownership. Meidner is today remembered much more as a proponent of this radical idea than for his work on the labour market – the battle over wage-earner funds left deep scars. Fuelled by arguments such as this, the consensus between unions and business began to disintegrate.

By the early 1980s, the atmosphere of consensus and collaboration between unions and employers had been replaced by a "full-blown confrontation regime", wrote Nils Elvander, one of Sweden's foremost political economists. The relationship that had shaped Swedish industry for 40 years was now in crisis. The engineers union broke away from central bargaining to strike a separate deal with employers. A few years later, the employers federation SAF closed down its central bargaining unit altogether. Meanwhile, SAF was mobilising against the unions, and in 1983 organised a demonstration of 75,000 people in Stockholm against the wage-earner funds and "socialism".

Things came to a head in 1990, when the bursting of a debt bubble sparked a deep recession, bankrupting the banks and inflicting the worst economic shock Sweden had experienced since the 1930s. In three years, public debt doubled, unemployment tripled, and the government's deficit increased 10-fold. A newspaper front page showed a picture of a newborn child with the headline: "Born with a debt of 150,000 Swedish krona". The country elected its first unashamedly free-market government, determined to put an end to the years of Social Democratic excess. Newspapers and journals across the world proclaimed the end of the Swedish model. In the midst of the crisis, Meidner himself surveyed the wreckage: "The Swedish system, balancing private ownership and social control, has broken down," he wrote.

The early 1990s was a period when social democracy was in disarray internationally. In the minds of many, the collapse of the Soviet bloc heralded "the end of history" and the triumph of liberal capitalism. Governments raced to distance themselves from what was seen as outdated ideology, replacing state ownership with privatisation while pursing tax cuts and free markets for labour and public services. This transformation was repeated in Sweden, where the Social Democrats were defeated in the polls and then returned to office – but with a programme to continue the deregulation and privatisation started by the interim Conservative government.

Sweden's business environment started to converge with the rest of Western Europe. Electricity, telephones, railways and the post office were privatised, while Sweden's system of vouchers and choice in secondary education became a model for economic liberals across the world. Academics interviewed for this book talked about a demoralisation and even despair among Swedish Social Democrats at the time, who lost faith in classic centre-left policies. Successive Social Democratic governments cut back on the active labour market policies that had helped maintain skills and ease the transition between jobs.

However, obituaries for the Swedish model were premature. Unions and employers, ubiquitously referred to in Sweden as the "social partners", had walked away from each other. But behind the scenes, efforts were soon afoot to put Humpty Dumpty together again – despite a global context that em-

> The Grand Hotel in Saltsjöbaden, where an agreement between employers and trade unions laid the basis for Sweden's long-lasting consensus approach to labour relations.

phasised free market solutions to just about everything. In fact, economic necessity drove them back into each other's arms.

Swedish business was struggling to grow. Employers were failing to curb a new wage-price spiral – in 1995, despite the highest unemployment since the 1930s, strikes broke out and the average salary increase was above the EU average, after the booming forestry industry set a high benchmark for other sectors. This was a watershed year. Major Swedish export companies, which a decade earlier had been the driving force behind destroying the system of centralised wage negotiation, now changed tack. At the same time, the government prodded union leaders to reach out to employers and put their differences aside. The focus had to be on strengthening Sweden's competitiveness, without which there could be no wage rises in the longer term.

A leap of the imagination was required. The resulting agreement between the two sides of Swedish industry, signed in March 1997, lacked inspiration only in its title: the Industry Agreement. Almost 60 years since the famous Saltsjöbaden deal that set the tone for three decades of industrial peace, employers and unions signed a document on "industrial development and wage formation" that set out a shared vision for creating a sound economy that

55

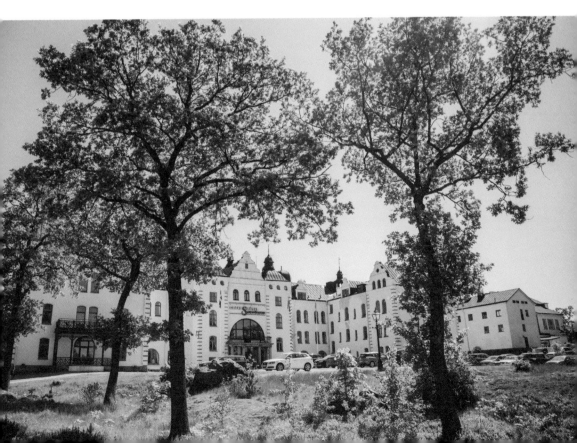

could deliver rising living standards. A virtuous circle could be re-started that delivered real-terms wage rises without fuelling inflation or unemployment, the agreement stated, while strengthening the competitive position of Swedish industry by developing workers' competence and skills.

In contrast with Saltsjöbaden, widely seen by the outside world as a cornerstone of the Swedish model after the War, the Industry Agreement has no such reputation – and indeed is largely unheard of beyond Sweden. However, the Agreement marks not only continuity with 1938, but its rescue and resurrection after two decades of industrial strife. And in the eyes of close observers of Swedish economic history such as Elvander, it ended the confrontation regime and ushered in a new era of cooperation. The importance of personal trust between the two sides is an outstanding feature: they identify areas of common interest, disagreements are neither swept under the carpet nor exaggerated, and the relationship is – most of the time – characterised by sincerity and integrity.

Meanwhile, the government established an agency, the Swedish National Mediation Office, to keep the agreement on the rails. The Mediation Office is a body unique to Sweden; its task is to find solutions that avoid conflict, but within strict limits set by the needs of the country's export-oriented sectors. This new flowering of collaboration means that, 20 years after the ink dried on the agreement, wage norms are set centrally for 90 per cent of the labour market.

The tensions between employers and unions that built up in the 1970s and broke out into a bare-knuckle fight in the 80s marked an "extreme crisis" in the Swedish labour market model, says Anders Weihe, chief negotiator for the engineering employers federation, who has been at the heart of negotiations with the unions since 1998. Looking back, he says:

"Did we put Humpty Dumpty back together again? More or less. Our core issue was international competitiveness. The same thinking was behind the cooperation between unions and employers in the 1940s-60s, when industry was working well and it was extremely important to have industrial peace. Collective bargaining is a very effective instrument – if you have knowledgeable people who are not overloaded with ideology, you can create a system where wage formation works."

'LUBRICATION FOR THE LABOUR MARKET'

The system has its ups and downs. In 2010 the engineering employers briefly withdrew because they believed that wage rises were undermining competitiveness. Also, centralised pay bargaining means that any booming sector has to hold back wage increases, even if it can afford to pay more and therefore poach more workers. But so far, employers in such sectors, such as construction, have stuck to the belief that in the long term the Industry Agreement will serve them better than any short-term gains offered by breaking free from it.

There was rare glimpse of employer discord in 2007, when shop workers and employers agreed on a rather high pay increase, but the employers organisation stepped in to rap some knuckles and have the deal annulled. Moreover, the central agreements have gradually evolved in a direction that allows for more local differences in wages. A typical collective agreement merely designs a "pot" that the employer has to implement on average, but not for all individuals. While this has had a measurable effect, a defining feature of Swedish wages remains their flatness, and the relative equality of income across the economy.

But what happened to helping workers in inefficient companies who were made redundant because their employers cannot cut wages? As we saw above, the purpose of Sweden's unusual model of wage bargaining is to maintain the productivity of the economy overall, which in turn requires a well-functioning "transition system" whereby those who lose their jobs can move quickly into other sectors. With the government's gradual exit from active labour market policy, the job security agencies have been left to take up the slack.

When I meet Johan Sandgren, an advisor at the offices of the white-collar TRR job security agency in central Stockholm, I expect to find him stressed and exhausted – Ericsson, the Swedish telecoms equipment maker, had recently announced thousands redundancies, and Sandgren was the responsible official at TRR. Jobless Ericsson workers turned to TRR for help in their droves, two-thirds of them in Stockholm. But Sandgren was serene. "It is what we do all the time, so we didn't feel that stressed. We had to employ extra counsellors and open more offices, but it is normal for us," he said.

Ericsson's troubles have seen the company make several rounds of redundancies over the past decade, so TRR knew what to expect. In 2017–18, many workers took redundancy voluntarily, with a financial package. There was a lot of rumours and negativity surrounding the company and many were tired of working there anyway, said Sandgren, who had been addressing meetings

"WE GET PEOPLE TO FEEL THEY HAVE VALUE, A PLACE IN THE MARKET, TO HAVE SELF-BELIEF. WE COMPLEMENT OUR COUNSELLING WITH A LOT OF THERAPY, THE FIGURES FOR PSYCHOLOGICAL AND PHYSICAL UNHEALTHY ARE GROWING. WORK RELATED STRESS IS A REASON – COMPANIES ARE DOWN-SIZING AND PEOPLE ARE DOING MORE."

Johan Sandgren, *job security advisor TRR*

of hundreds of Ericsson workers since the redundancies were announced. The jobs market for skilled engineers was favourable, so their prospects were good. "You can almost feel the difference when you stand on a stage in front of people who are hoping for a new future," Sandgren said.

TRR was established in the mid-1970s when restructuring started to hit white-collar jobs. Unions and employers realised they needed something more than the government-run jobless centres, which were focused on blue-collar workers and the long-term unemployed. Now almost 98 per cent of all white-collar workers facing redundancy come to TRR. If you are an engineer at Ericsson focusing on telecoms production that has now moved to Asia, you might need some training to take a job in IT, for example. TRR has funds for that. If you are a programmer and you don't have the latest skills, TRR can do it. On-the-job training is quite common in big companies, but it rarely has certification – TRR can help with that too.

Then there is the counselling that Gunilla Stensson found so useful. When employers handle redundancies badly, it hits people's self-confidence. The combination of a long period at the same employer and shoddy treatment during the transition is a particularly damaging mix: you only know that your competence is good within the company, you don't know your market value, and you are in bad shape to face the future. Sandgren said:

"We get people to feel they have value, a place in the market, to have self-belief. We complement our counselling with a lot of therapy – we know that psychological and physical ill-health are growing, and work related stress is a reason. Companies are downsizing and people are doing more. Also people are becoming more aware of stress. At TRR people can open up, for the first time they can talk about how they feel."

The 2008 financial crisis also had the effect of encouraging smaller IT and telecoms companies to join the system, Sandgren said, because they realised it was easier for them to manage things through a collective agreement with the unions. "Before the crisis it was rare for small and middle sized IT companies to have a collective agreement with the unions – now it is common. You have an agreement, it is easier to see what's going happen," Sandgren said. "Also it can be good to do so as a branding thing, you are seen as a more solid company, which is a big advantage if you want to attract the right people." All the same, when Sandgren visited companies, it was common that half the workers in the audience didn't know they had protection from TRR, and were delighted when they realised they were entitled to it.

This is a largely hidden part of Sweden's welfare system that people only find out about when they are laid off. And because it is away from the public eye, there are few statistics and even fewer studies of how it works. "Sweden's welfare state today can come out rather poorly in comparisons with other countries, but this system doesn't show up in those studies," says Lars Walter, associate professor of management at Gothenburg University's Business School, and one of the few academics to have studied the job security agencies. "There is no legislation, it is not public policy, but it is really important – it is such a unique phenomenon," he says. His research on the agencies found them to be very efficient, which explains why they have grown – they work well, the basic premise is sound, and 80 per cent of laid-off workers are back in a job within a year. But nobody planned it, there is no oversight, and nobody knows exactly what its consequences are for society as a whole. "It is a system that just happened," professor Walters says.

Indeed, Sweden's transition system has no equivalents in Europe. According to Lennard Hedström, the head of TRR, the transition system is "lubrication for the labour market":

"It is easier to make someone redundant if you know that they will get professional support. If you look at bigger companies, it is easier to make people redundant in Sweden compared to most European countries. There

60

is much less regulation around redundancy here, because we have the collective agreements. The combination of supplementary unemployment benefit and coaching is what works. It takes the stress out of being made redundant. And we are not an official agency; we are more of a private company, owned by the unions and employers. Transition agreements, and the job security agencies like ours, are part of the Swedish model."

Ultimately, the job security agencies don't create any vacancies. In the event that job creation should dry up, no amount of interview role-playing or confidence building will get people back into work. But 45 years since the first agencies were established, the system still works, and works well. "In the 70s the ideas were totally different," says TRR's Johan Sandgren. "But time has shown that this old model still fits, both on an individual and company level. It's a solid part of society. The biggest reason for this to fly is that everyone is happy with it."

'IT ALLOWS PEOPLE TO DARE'

So what does Swedish business think of a system in which companies cannot pay their workers what they want? For many major industrialists, the gains outweigh the disadvantages. Leif Johansson, who has held leadership roles on companies such as Volvo, Ericsson, Electrolux and AstraZeneca, believes the Industry Agreement was a "milestone" that has prevented hostile moves by both unions and employers, while ensuring that the competitiveness of Sweden's exporters has not been damaged by high wage settlements in other parts of the economy. The framework has been surprisingly successful at setting the salary benchmark for the rest of Swedish industry, while making it difficult for "populistic" companies that want to drive down costs and wages, he says:

"This is a mechanism in which disputes are handled by independent mediators, it makes strikes and lockouts a last resort. The institutions of the Industry Agreement have been strong enough to make it difficult for aggressive employers or unions to do something dramatically different. It sounds like a rather rosy picture of how wonderful Sweden is. But when you run a country like this that is exposed, as we are, to international competition, of course there are tensions. However, at a national level we have made it stick."

"THE 'SPECIAL RELATIONSHIP' WITH THE UNIONS IS BASED ON AN UNDERSTANDING THAT SWEDISH INDUSTRY NEEDS CONSTANTLY TO ADAPT AND CHANGE. SO WE HAVE BUILT A FLEXIBLE SYSTEM TO MEET GLOBALISATION IN THE RIGHT WAY."

Carl Bennet, *industrialist and investor*

62

For Carl Bennet, billionaire industrialist and investor, the "special relationship" with the unions is based on an understanding that Swedish industry needs constantly to adapt and change. This is a flexible system that fits the demands of globalisation:

> *"With that system we have an attitude towards globalisation that is not negative — people are always questioning changes, but we have a social system that gives the possibility to go from one job to another and have a certain security during this time. Consequently, people are not so scared about what might happen to them when they lose their jobs, and they are more prepared to adjust. The Swedish model handles this in a good way because we have created a social system that gives flexibility, so we can go from one situation to another without having a lot of strikes. We are adjusting better than many other countries."*

High wages also force companies to be innovative, says Stina Ehrensvärd, Swedish American entrepreneur and founder of high-tech company Yubico. In the US, she says, low wages have not made the country more efficient. "Instead, people sit and do really simple tasks," she says. "High salaries have forced us in Sweden to automate, to use technology. That is one of the good side effects of having high salaries – we fully embraced the internet as a way to automate. When we started Yubico we felt like that too, it all had to be au-

"WE NEED TO KEEP PEOPLE EMPLOYABLE AND KEEP THEIR KNOWLEDGE UP TO DATE, BECAUSE SWEDEN NEEDS ALL THE ENGINEERS WE CAN GET."

Jane Walerud, *investor in Sweden*

tomated, this was in our mindset. And because of that we have been able to lower the costs more than if we were manufacturing things in Asia, because using robots is even cheaper."

Another example of this mechanism in action is Stockholm's innovative financial technology, or fintech, scene, according to Pär Hedberg, founder of STING, Stockholm Innovation and Growth, a business incubator for some of the capital's most promising start-ups:

> *"The minimum salary you can pay here is much higher than in other countries, and as a result, many large companies are forced to rationalise and be extremely competitive. We have four or five big banks here, they are extremely cost-effective compared to other countries, because they have been forced to use new technology earlier, which has led to a spinning out of companies from the innovative banking sector."*

Hedberg sees a further positive aspect of Sweden's broader social welfare system – it fosters an entrepreneurial culture. An advantage of having a welfare safety net is that if you fail, you are not forced to lose your home. "It allows people to dare," he says. Niklas Adalberth, co-founder of Klarna, a hugely successful fintech start-up, says Sweden's welfare provision was an additional incentive for him to pursue his entrepreneurial goals as a student, even though he had little experience beyond flipping burgers: "The worst thing that could happen was maybe I would have a one or two-year gap in my CV, which no-one really cares about."

Jane Walerud, the American investor we have met before, agrees. If you are a entrepreneur in the US and you have a spouse and children, you need expensive health insurance. If your child has a bike accident, you are in trouble. So in the US entrepreneurs are very young, they have no responsibilities. "Here in Sweden, if someone gets hurt it makes no difference; if the company goes bad, you are still okay," Walerud says. "So I get to invest with 40-year-old entrepreneurs who know their stuff, who know their industry. Can you imagine being 40 in the States and doing that?"

Indeed, Silicon Valley seems to be oblivious to the value of experience. The average age of entrepreneurs supported by Y-Combinator, a company that invests in thousands of tech startups in the valley, is 29. Sweden, by contrast, recognises the cost to society of making 45-year-olds feel as if they can no longer contribute. "We need to keep people employable and keep their knowledge up to date, because Sweden needs all the engineers we can get," Walerud says. It is relatively easy to recruit British engineers to work in Sweden, she adds, because the UK doesn't value them that the way it should.

One consequence of the system's focus on skills and competitiveness is that Sweden has a relatively small share of low-skilled adults, and at the same time a pool of highly-skilled people, with a strong participation rate in adult learning. This makes the country better prepared than others to benefit from globalisation, says the OECD. Swedish workers have literacy, numeracy and problem solving skills well above the OECD average, plus some of the highest readiness to learn.

However, it is a constant battle to ensure the nation's skill set matches its economic needs. It is not the supply of competent people so much as the supply of the right sort of competencies, says Pontus Braunerhjelm, professor of international business and entrepreneurship at Stockholm's Royal Institute of Technology. Many more Swedes today have university education, for example, but there is an increasing mismatch between the output of the country's universities and the needs of the economy. "Labour training and retraining – the possibility to be part of a labor market programme that increases your chances of being employed again – has diminished quite substantially," professor Braunerhjelm says.

Consequently, an important issue in coming years will be the system for training people who are in work, according to Anders Ferbe, head of the engineers union IF Metall. "We have to prioritise skills," he says. "I have discussed this a lot with the employers' organisations, and we still haven't found a system for doing it. We need to use the Swedish model for the new circumstances, and competencies is a key word for the future."

Let's leave the final word to one of the more remarkable phenomena to have emerged from the resurrected Rehn-Meidner model – the TCO, the huge and fast-growing white-collar trade union we met in Chapter 1. Between 2006 and 2011, Sweden lost 450,000 jobs to automation – roughly 90,000 every year, or 2.5 per cent of the workforce. But the TCO leadership hasn't blinked. Eva Nordmark, the TCO's leader, says:

"I am in favour of that because we have strong social dialogue and strong welfare. When I was interviewed by some French journalists about the transatlantic trade negotiations a few years ago, they could not understand how a union leader in Sweden can be so positive to free trade when everyone else is so against it. My answer was that collectively bargained transition support systems mean that if you lose your job you don't have to be poor, and you get support to find new work. The same is true when digitalisation leads to structural change. You shouldn't be marginalised if you lose your job. This is important not just for each of my members, but for the whole of society."

SUMMARY CHAPTER 2

We are getting to know our Swedish bumblebee a bit better.
To sum up:

- Swedish businesses pay a portion of their turnover into "job security agencies", which help workers who are made redundant.

- These agencies emerged out of a unique, centralised wage bargaining between unions and employers, the aim of which is to force Swedish industry to remain internationally competitive through constantly innovating and restructuring.

- This framework relied on strong mutual trust and cooperation between unions and employers, but this collapsed in the 1980s.

- Many believed this was the end of the Swedish model. But the need to keep wages under control saw unions and employers put Humpty Dumpty back together again.

- Today, the job security agencies lubricate the economy by taking the sting out of large-scale restructuring and job losses.

- Business leaders say that Sweden's strong welfare safety net has an additional benefit, in so far as it takes some of the risk out of entre-preneurship, encouraging people to dare to pursue business ideas.

CHAPTER 3

'THE 100 YEAR PLAN':
THE LURE OF THE
LONG TERM

IKEA's store at the end of the earth; what it tells us about Ingvar Kamprad's views on economics; what is different about the way Swedish owners run their companies; the broader philosophy of Swedish capitalism; rising wealth, rising inequality?

In the autumn of 2012, a Canadian delegation arrived in the far north of Sweden to talk about the Arctic. They found themselves in Haparanda, a small town at the northern apex of the leaden, elongated sea that stretches south, separating Scandinavia proper from Finland to the east. They were surprised to find that this remote corner of the planet had not gone unnoticed by history – their hotel boasted that spies, sawmill barons, army officers, noblemen and brothel madams had all enjoyed its hospitality. In 1908, the US explorer Robert Peary purchased furs in the town for the first expedition to reach the North Pole. In April 1917, Lenin arrived in Haparanda by train, taking a sledge over the frozen river into Finland and onwards to lead the revolution in Russia. Thomas Cook, founder of the travel company that still bears his name, declared that a "true globetrotter" must visit the tomb of Tamerlane in Samarkand, the ancient mosques of Timbuktu, and... Haparanda. For the record, I have not (yet) been to any of these places.

The Canadian visitors were unimpressed, however. "We were quite sceptical looking around Haparanda, which was a town with no one in the streets," the

> Let's go to IKEA... Sweden's far north is remote and sparsely populated.

delegation's leader reported. At least it had roads, she noted, unlike a lot of northern communities in Canada. Once a busy port, Haparanda's industries such as timber and fishing were "dying off". She spied one bright spot among the region's prospects: "The town is still alive because an IKEA has been built, and it's where all the Russians come across Finland to buy their IKEA products. I'm not sure that putting IKEAs into all northern communities in Canada would have the same success, but you can see that innovation is being used to try to come up with ways to keep a community alive."

The story of the world's northernmost IKEA sheds a little more light on the way Sweden runs its free market economy. Naturally it involves the store's founder, Ingvar Kamprad, the late billionaire, tax exile and folk hero who erected a little piece of Scandinavia in so many households across the globe, in the shape of a self-assembly bookshelf or bathroom storage unit. It was 2003, and the newly elected Social Democratic mayor of Haparanda, Sven-Erik Bucht, was aware of speculation in the newspapers that IKEA wanted to build a store in the far north. The following year, Bucht learned that Kamprad would make a public appearance in the capital, so he flew to Stockholm and buttonholed him. The three-minute encounter between the world's fourth richest man and the left-wing councillor from Haparanda has become a legend.

Bucht succeeded in planting the seed of an idea in Kamprad's mind, which somehow took root and grew. It became known as "Ingvar's project" – his plan to build a huge new store in Haparanda, effectively in the middle of nowhere. The entire board of IKEA was firmly against it, Kamprad confessed, because they couldn't see how it could make any money – Haparanda broke all the rules, IKEA stores needed a large population within a certain radius. But Kamprad pressed on. After the opening of the Haparanda IKEA in 2006, he explained that he and Bucht simply "fell in love".

In the town itself there was euphoria. One of its oldest residents told a radio station that IKEA coming here was the best thing that's happened to Haparanda in the 90 years he had lived there. The town's economy briefly became the fastest growing in Sweden, house prices soared and unemployment evaporated. Haparanda declared it wanted to become a "eurocity" where shoppers could use either euros or Swedish crowns, and it was touted as a model for Swedish advocates of eurozone membership. Bucht was named Swede of the Year for halting the region's slow economic demise.

There was more to Kamprad's thinking than a romantic attachment to Sweden's remote north. His decision was based on similar reasoning behind taking the brand to a handful of depopulated areas in Sweden where he believed a store would have a positive economic effect. "There must be a helping hand for all the young people who do not thrive so well in the cities, but who would rather experience our wonderful nature. We must give them a chance," he told the press. "I see it as a social mission – I turn to the many with thin wallets." About the opposition from IKEA's board, he said:

"The younger generation is more interested in America or China or Japan or Italy and all that, but I am an old man who thinks we are doing a good job here at home [in Sweden]. ... I think the era of old-fashioned capitalism, jungle capitalism, is over and it will be replaced by a modern and responsible market economy that takes a greater degree of social responsibility."

The Kamprad family privately owns IKEA – it keeps its finances to itself, so it is impossible to know whether the investment in Haparanda has paid off. The store claims more than 1.5 million visitors annually from Sweden, Finland, Norway and Russia. But it is not just the younger members of IKEA's board who thought Kamprad was crazy to invest there. "Of course it is not profitable," a very senior Swedish investor told me in Stockholm, complaining that the company's private ownership meant it could go against the strict rules of the market without being punished on the stock market. "Kamprad could do that as a private company, a public company could not, it has to follow the rules. Kamprad doesn't have to. The day he passes away they will sell it," the investor said, asking not to be named.

Indeed, the IKEA effect did not appear to be permanent. By 2017 unemployment had climbed back up to 15 per cent, and Haparanda topped the list of Swedish towns for residents receiving jobless benefits. The company sold off the shopping centre it owned adjacent to the Haparanda store, because it didn't fit with a vision of creating "communities" around its malls.

The story of the IKEA store in Haparanda begs many questions. Was it just the whim of an old man with more money than sense? Or does it tell us something broader about the relationship between economy and society? Does Sweden really make a priority of "the people with thin wallets", putting social responsibility above the laws of "jungle capitalism"? Politicians would never deny that people come before profits, but what do Sweden's biggest capitalists say?

Before we search for answers, we must look briefly at a peculiar feature of how Swedish industry is owned and controlled. In international business circles, Sweden has a reputation for encouraging long-term ownership of companies through good times and bad. This stands in contrast to the shorter-term outlook inherent in the so-called "Anglo-Saxon model" of capitalism, which allegedly emphasises short-term profits at the expense of long-term

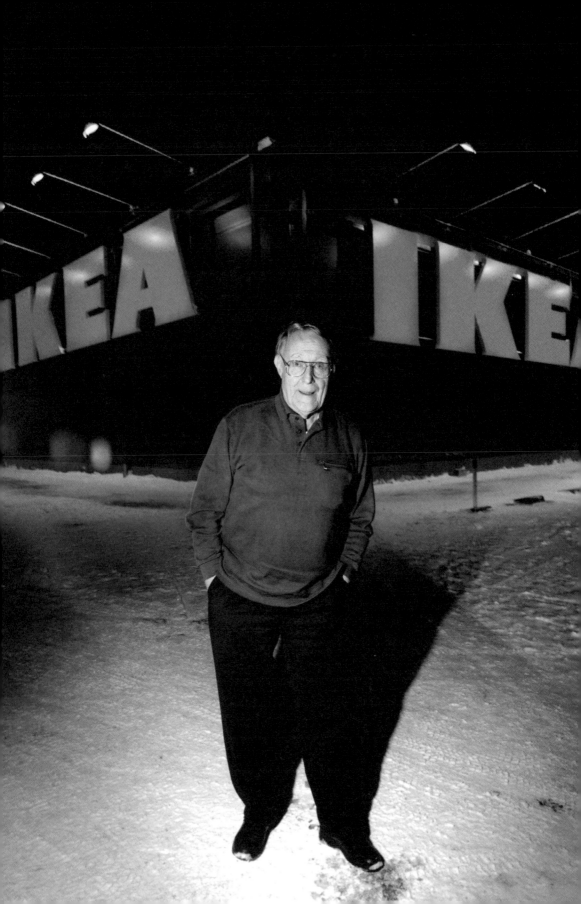

"THERE MUST BE A HELPING HAND FOR ALL THE YOUNG PEOPLE WHO DO NOT THRIVE SO WELL IN THE CITIES, BUT WHO WOULD RATHER EXPERIENCE OUR WONDERFUL NATURE. WE MUST GIVE THEM A CHANCE."

IKEA's late founder Ingvar Kamprad at the store in Haparanda

planning. The Anglo-Saxon approach also combines lower taxes, looser regulation, a weaker social safety net, and greater ease for firms to hire and fire employees. At business level, it puts the interests of shareholders above those of other stakeholders, such as employees.

In Sweden it works like this. The bulk of the economy is controlled by large investment organisations – some of them owned by powerful families – with a track record of owning and managing companies for decades, so a long-term philosophy is hard-wired into their thinking. This is further encouraged by an unusual system of "dual class" share ownership, also known as A and B shares, which gives some shareholders a bigger stake in the company if they commit for the longer term. Owners of A shares, which are more expensive, have much more say over how the company is managed, so that even a minority shareholding can mean dominance over a company's long-term direction.

This is a Swedish model of "active ownership", where shareholders are expected to exercise their power over the long term, rather than just looking to bail out if they think management is likely to damage the share price. After the financial crash of 2008, in which short-term, get-rich-quick thinking appeared to play a role, this model attracted attention internationally among governments and regulators seeking to avoid another slump. But does it work? And how has long-term thinking, if that's what it is, shaped the kind of economy that Sweden has created?

'BUY TO BUILD, NOT BUY TO SELL'

In 2011, Keith McLoughlin, a senior US executive, was appointed boss of Electrolux, the giant Swedish maker of washing machines and refrigerators. He wanted to hit the ground running with a plan for his first 100 days – a period for which new governments, presidents and business chiefs are commonly assessed. But for McLoughlin, this would be a lesson. He recalls:

"When I was first appointed I thought it would be good to interview every director on the board individually. I got through three or four of them, all Swedes, asking for their input on the issues and opportunities, and shared with them my main issues for my 100 day plan. But there were puzzled looks and furrowed brows – I could tell the interviews were not going well. Then this guy said: 'I want to give you a tip. For a Swedish director to hear about a 100 day plan makes us very nervous. We want to hear about your 100 year plan.'"

For the new boss, his colleagues' reaction was unnerving. But he came to see the long-term outlook as a positive feature, McLoughlin says. Instead of judging progress purely in terms of the next quarterly report to the market, which reacts by praising or punishing management's performance through the share price, he could look beyond short-term setbacks in favour of sustainable long-term goals. He says:

"The whole quarterly thing with a publicly traded company doesn't always create the most value for the shareholder. The vast majority of shareholders in the US hold shares for under a year. So their time window and horizon gives them a very different perspective from someone who is holding the share for the long term, who wants to be certain that every decision is adding value, someone who doesn't worry about the short-term gyrations. If you hold stock for less than a year it is all about the gyrations."

Richard Twomey, a broad-chested Welshman who has spent decades at the top of big life-science companies, was based in California when he got the call to swap surf and sunshine for the grey skies of Gothenburg. He took over a company with an unpronounceable name that is nonetheless a world leader in manufacturing medical products: Mölnlycke Healthcare. When my mother was being nursed in the last months of her life in a small town on England's south coast, it was dressings made by Mölnlycke Healthcare that helped to heal the frequent tears in her delicate skin – a connection with my new home town that my family discovered only after her death.

Twomey's initial reaction to Scandinavia was not positive, he told the *Financial Times*. "Sweden, you have got to be joking. Cold and wet, and there's no surf." For Twomey, a keen surfer, this was a problem. But a determining factor for Twomey was the company's long-term outlook. His experience of working in US companies was the quarterly pressure to deliver results, so the long-term strategy became the next three months. In Sweden, by contrast, investors hold on for the long term. "If you want to be a CEO this is a dream environment in which to do it. A big reason I came here was the ownership," he says.

What is more, Twomey was wrong about the surf. A stretch of sand 30 minutes to the south of Gothenburg delivers reasonable waves after a windy night. When I met him at the company's HQ, Twomey was already anticipating a 5pm getaway for the beach. But first he found time to explain how the long-term perspective was a "conservative and very sensible" way to run industry:

> *"If you've got to sum up Swedish business and industry, that's pretty much what makes it different. The mechanics are much the same everywhere, in terms of systems, processes and approach to the market. The difference is when you have an ownership structure like Investor, the owners of Mölnlycke Healthcare. Look at Swedish corporate giants SKF, Volvo, Atlas Copco – they are very well run businesses that are managed for the long term. ... There is a certain patience here. When you are running it for the long term it is a dream environment. You put a plan in place and you have complete understanding and alignment with the owners and the board."*

77

If a company is hit by crisis, the model allows time to address the problem and implement a well planned transition that is not driven by short-term market considerations, Twomey believes. He sees only one equivalent in the Anglo-Saxon business sphere: the US investment company Berkshire Hathaway, run by US investment guru Warren Buffet, which also seeks to buy good companies, put competent management in place and invest for the long term.

In Sweden, major shareholders don't panic over a quarterly result that isn't up to expectations, according to Stu Graham, a US executive who spent 26 years at the top of Skanska, the Swedish multinational construction group, including six years as CEO. "As a result of that, it is very good for management to be able to pursue a longer-term agenda," he says. The long-term owners insist on results, so it is not the case that the set-up takes the heat off management. They hold our feet to the fire," Graham says. "But it is a very comforting way of doing business."

Skanska's main shareholder is an investment company called Industrivärden, while Mölnlycke is controlled by the Wallenbergs' Investor group. Together, these two "holding companies" – which hold onto the shares of other companies, rather than producing goods or services themselves – control more than half the Swedish economy. The overriding aim when buying stakes in companies is "buy to build, not buy to sell", says Johan Forssell, CEO of Investor. Investor holds controlling stakes in 18 Swedish companies. "Our strategy is to work with them and develop them as if we are going to own them for 50 years or longer," he says, sitting in Investor's ornate offices close to the Royal Gardens near Stockholm's central waterfront.

If Investor wished to make a profit from selling off the company silver, there is no shortage of global companies who would like to buy any one of Investor's holdings. But for Forssell, doing so only creates short-term cash for Investor, rather than long-term value. His reasoning goes like this. When you buy a company, you hope it is a great performer, efficient and profitable, but you need to own it for a number of years before you can really know. If you sell it, you might get a good price, but then you need to buy another great company. That would mean paying a high price, but without detailed knowledge of its potential, which only comes after a few years of ownership. Lots of companies can look cheap on paper, Forssell says:

> "But often they won't turn out to be a cheap acquisition in 10 years time because they will perform poorly. If you pay a high price for a great company, leading the market in an attractive niche, in 10 years' time normally it will turn out to have been a great deal. If you have a three-year horizon you can be successful buying whatever you like. If you invest in a company and you plan to keep it for decades, you have to go for the good ones."

Like Twomey, Forssell is also a fan of Warren Buffett, who once said it is better to buy a wonderful company at a fair price than a fair company at a wonderful price. That aphorism sums up the Investor approach, Forssell says: "Strong long-term ownership is beneficial, it leads to improved company performance, I truly believe in it." Industrivärden, the other huge investment house that dominates Swedish business, professes to have the same approach. "It's important for every company to have one of a few big shareholders who take a long-term view and long-term responsibility," the group's chief, Fredrik Lundberg, told the *Financial Times* in a rare interview.

'I AM A LITTLE BIT SOCIALIST TOO'

From the perspective of this book, does this approach to business count as another Swedish "bumblebee" – something that really ought not to fly, but still manages to get off the ground? Dual class shares are not exclusive to Sweden. When Google went public in 2004, its founders, Larry Page and Sergey Brin, insisted on a dual-class share structure so that, with around one-fifth of Google's total shares, the founders still commanded about three-fifths of votes, and thus retained control. Google made dual class shares fashionable again in North America. So Facebook's dual-class model gives company founder Mark Zuckerberg less than 1 per cent of the social-media giant's publicly traded stock and 60 per cent of its voting rights. Sweden is merely the European country in which the practice is most widespread: some two-thirds of its stock market listed companies have them.

The ownership structure of the bulk of Swedish industry is a key element of the Swedish model, according to Mats Andersson, a senior Swedish financier. Andersson says he became aware of its uniqueness when he became the CEO of AP4, one of Sweden's massive national pension funds, where for more than decade from the mid-2000s he was responsible for investing Swedes' pension contributions. Under the Anglo-Saxon model of capitalism, he says, ownership is fragmented and shareholders are largely passive, not interested in how managers run the company:

79

"They leave the work of good governance to others, they are free riders, their only driver is to drive down costs. We all know markets are not perfect, therefore I am an advocate of active management of money. The important ingredient is to make owners accountable, make sure they are active and responsible. In a world where investors are becoming more short-term oriented as we speak, we need more long-term investors. Sweden has been extremely lucky to have the ownership model combined with responsible families that own companies for the long term. It is a pretty unique system, and it has served us extremely well."

Andersson points to the fact that the Swedish stock exchange has consistently outperformed the MSCI World share index by 5 to 7 per cent over the past 20 years.

The dual-class share model, with more power for those who commit for the long term, is an "oddity" that is peculiar to Sweden, says Björn Wahlroos, Finland's leading businessman and Chairman of Sweden's largest bank, Nordea. But its importance is waning, he says, as more and more shares in Swedish

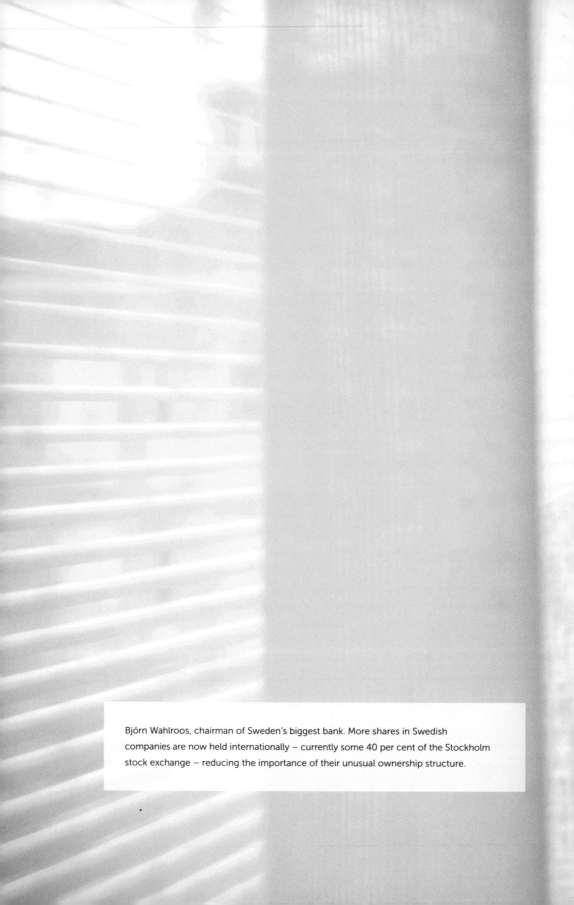

Björn Wahlroos, chairman of Sweden's biggest bank. More shares in Swedish companies are now held internationally – currently some 40 per cent of the Stockholm stock exchange – reducing the importance of their unusual ownership structure.

"THE DUAL-CLASS SHARE MODEL, WITH MORE POWER FOR THOSE WHO COMMIT FOR THE LONG TERM, IS AN 'ODDITY' THAT IS PECULIAR TO SWEDEN."

Björn Wahlroos, *Finland's leading business figure*

82   companies are owned internationally – currently some 40 per cent of the Stockholm stock exchange. It has had one demonstrable positive effect: Swedish industry has invested more in Sweden, Wahlroos says. But it is no panacea:

> *"Is this a good idea? The libertarian in me says be my guest, and there are many, like the Wallenbergs, who attach a lot of importance to it. But the Wallenbergs have come under a lot of criticism for being inactive in their holdings – the debate over Investor is that they are not active enough."*

Some at the top of Swedish industry go further than the long-term perspective. For them, running companies means more than just better business performance – it is also an element of a broader philosophy that stresses the need to spread the benefits from business throughout society, rather than concentrate them among a wealthy few. On paper, Carl Bennet is one of Sweden's wealthiest men, having successful invested in Swedish medical technology and the life sciences. He has been on the board of global healthcare equipment maker Getinge for almost 30 years. The long-term perspective gives society a much more solid way to ensure that everyone benefits, Bennet says:

*"The short-term philosophy is extremely egoistic, and when it domi-
nates you don't have a balance, you can run into big problems because it
favours only a small part of society."*

From inside a glass-walled eyrie perched high – like his principles? – on a
vaulting rock above Slottsskogen park in Gothenburg, Bennet cannot get
enough of the long term. He complains that Sweden has lost control of some
important companies because their owners preferred to sell them off. He
himself is approached every year by competitors who want to purchase the
companies he controls, but for Bennet it is not about feathering his own nest,
but rather "a life-long journey" to develop these businesses:

*"With a long-term perspective you are making sure it will benefit society as
such. With a short-term approach, you get in, do your best, take money
and go away; you are stepping into a business in order to abandon it, to
make a big profit. You go in to get out. If you are in for the long term, you
don't maximise things for the benefit of yourself and a few others. Short-
sighted actions can make society vulnerable. If you just want to make as*

84

much profit as possible you leave behind a lot of people who question what you took and what you were thinking about – that creates difficult movements in society that can change it in a negative way."

On the contrary, running a business to develop it legitimates the capitalist system and the market economy, Bennet believes. His outlook has earned him a reputation as the "red baron", a capitalist who leans to the left. Bennett himself rejects the moniker. "I believe strongly in the market economy," he says. "I think we should develop the country and make sure we distribute the wealth in a way that it can benefit many people. You have to develop the economy so it benefits the whole society." There is an echo of this approach in the guiding principles of the Wallenberg family's approach to business, which involves the idea of landsgagneligt, or "benefiting the nation" (see Chapter 6). It feels rather like the old-fashioned attitude of a captain towards his vessel – you are with it to the last, and you would go down with it rather than jump in the lifeboat and abandon ship.

So-called "angel investor" Jane Walerud came to Sweden from the US in the early 1980s and married a Swede, so she knows the country closely. She describes herself as a serial entrepreneur, and is behind such huge Swedish business successes such as Tobii and Klarna. When I met her at SUP46, a startup cafe in central Stockholm, we were surrounded by people half our age. Walerud stood out from the caffeine-fuelled twenty-somethings for her steady gaze, soft voice and calm but forceful presence.

Talking about what makes Sweden different, she starts with the high levels of trust. This means deals can be done on a handshake, which brings down costs, she says, because you don't need so many detailed contracts and lawyers. But a big part of that trust stems from the fact that most people in business believe that others are out for the good of the whole organisation, not just themselves, Walerud says, and "that organisation can also be Sweden as a whole". This is a country where people don't expect others just to look after themselves:

"When I do business in the UK, often the reaction from the people I am doing business with is: you want to sell the company straight away, so I'm not going help you. I say no, we are trying to build a company, selling is not the goal. They just don't believe me, because in the UK the general idea is to get as rich as possible as quickly as possible, and not necessarily to contribute to society as a whole."

< Carl Bennet, biotech billionaire with a reputation as Sweden's "red baron".

85

"WE HAVE DIFFERENT PRIORITIES BUT WE STILL AGREE TO A GREAT EXTENT ABOUT THE WAY WE WANT SWEDEN TO DEVELOP. THIS IS LOYALTY TO THE COMMUNITY BECAUSE THIS IS WHERE WE LIVE."

Jane Walerud, investor

Walerud sits on the country's National Innovation Council, chaired by the prime minister. Although she is on the right in Swedish political terms, she has been pushing an idea that will give more power to the trade unions. She says:

"That's just me contributing to the society, and everyone expects that I will. We need people to feel that we are looking out for them. We are all coming from the same place, we share the same reference, we agree approximately about where Sweden is. We have different priorities but we still agree to a great extent about the way we want Sweden to develop. This is loyalty to the community because this is where we live."

Seen in this light, perhaps Ingvar Kamprad's willingness to build an IKEA in Haparanda makes a little more sense. IKEA's Anders Moberg, who we met in Chapter 1, is not scared to use the 'S' word. Kamprad, he says, "was a capitalist but very much socialist in his way of being and acting. One dimension was business, but there was also a social dimension." Kamprad's approach seems to have rubbed off on Moberg:

"I am a little bit socialist too. It is a dimension you cannot ignore, you need to take a social responsibility for what you are doing. If we don't pay attention to this we will get a very divided world. The United States is the worst example. It is scary how divided countries are. In the mission of IKEA to sell

good design at affordable prices, already you have a very social approach. You can make money on that, but not on every piece you sell. You need to be there for the many in order to do it."

LIMITS TO LAGOM: WEALTH AND INEQUALITY

I confess that when wealthy business people start to bang on about the common good – let alone "socialism" – I find it hard not to raise an eyebrow. How serious is Sweden's capitalist class about redistribution? Is it just putting a self-serving gloss on the successful lining of its own pockets? The "we're all in this together", ties-off, first-name-terms approach we encountered earlier at IKEA might help to motivate middle managers, but it surely has its limits. Ingvar Kamprad moved to Switzerland in 1973 to avoid paying Swedish taxes, and relocated his company HQ to the Netherlands for the same reason. Kamprad largely got away with it – and his youthful membership of Sweden's Nazi movement – because Swedes basked in IKEA's global glory. Other wealthy Swedes have also jumped ship, such as Hans Rausing, billionaire scion of the Tetra Pak business, who fled the country's high taxes decades ago and moved his corporate HQ to Switzerland.

As we have seen, the long-term approach to investment, with its attendant notions of concern for a wider group rather than short-term personal gain, is hard wired into the Swedish system through the institution of dual class shares. Far more important, however, in terms of curbing animal instincts at the top of Swedish business, is a national culture in which public figures are subjected to minute scrutiny over their financial affairs. Famously, a former leader of the Social Democrats was forced to take a three year break from politics in the mid-1990s after it emerged she had used her government credit card to purchase personal items, including bars of Toblerone chocolate. A prosecutor's investigation found Mona Sahlin had broken no rules, but the "Toblerone affair" effectively prevented her from becoming Sweden's first female prime minister.

Swedish newspapers like nothing more than to question whether wealth is justified by performance. Following the Paradise Papers revelations about offshore accounts in 2017, investigative journalists calculated that Sweden loses more than €4 billion in tax revenue each year, or about 4 per cent of the government's annual spending – enough to pay the salaries of 100,000 nurses or educate 400,000 children – because of offshore tax avoidance by wealthy Swedes. Leif Östling, head of the Confederation of Swedish Enterprise and a former boss of truck-maker Scania, was forced to quit after it was revealed that he held several million euros in an offshore account, while private care companies within the Confederation relied on tax-payers money to make their profits.

In response to questions about his taxes, a visibly annoyed Östling blurted out: "What the hell do I get for my money?" a winged phrase that began trending on Twitter soon afterwards – each tweet banging another nail into Östling's coffin. Swedes were angry at his assumption that the super-rich have the right to take things into their own hands and buck the system. It offended their sense of lagom, that things should be "in moderation", or "just enough" – a sort of Goldilocks philosophy that holds that nothing in society should be too hot or too cold, but just right. It fell to the leader of Sweden's Conservatives, Ulf Kristersson, to point out to Östling: "This is not how it works in Sweden, nor is it going to work. You pay taxes on the basis of what you earn, you don't get back more from the state because you pay more taxes."

Sweden's executives were reminded of the lines they should not cross in 2015 when a scandal swept through some of the country's biggest companies, toppling some major names in one of the biggest shake-ups in Swedish boardroom history. It stemmed from newspaper revelations about corporate perks – namely that SCA, a pulp and paper company which is part of the Industrivärden empire, had flown executives to Formula One races, the World Cup and the Olympics. Attention focused on a hunting lodge built by the company on prime moose-hunting land in a remote and beautiful part of central Sweden, where potential business partners were entertained. Wives, children and pets accompanied directors on these trips.

An internal investigation found that none of the directors broke company policy, and it is hard to imagine executive behaviour of this nature making such big headlines in other countries, or having such a drastic impact. But the details made uncomfortable reading in a nation in which the sinews of social democracy are still more or less intact, despite being stretched and strained by neoliberalism since the early 1990s. The SCA scandal also exposed an incestuous system of cross-ownership, in which executives sat on many boards and approved each other's expenses. It led to a major clear-out of CEOs and chairmen from Swedish boards, as Industrivärden struggled to clean up the mess.

The revelations demonstrated a casual profligacy at the top of a country that feels uncomfortable with extravagance, lifting the lid on a secretive world of corporate perks in a society that has embraced globalisation but is hostile to ostentatious displays of wealth and privilege. Sweden's main business daily called on the country's capitalists to think about their legitimacy in the eyes of the wider population. The paper made a comparison between unelected executives and Sweden's royal family, whose popularity has also slipped in

89

IF SWEDEN CAN RESTORE ITS SENSE OF LAGOM AND HALT
THE TREND TOWARDS GROWING INEQUALITY, IT WILL
NOT JUST BE REVERTING TO HISTORICAL TYPE, BUT ALSO
SINGING IN TUNE WITH RECENT ECONOMIC THINKING.
THIS WILL DEMAND FAR-SIGHTED POLITICIANS LOOKING
TO THE LONG-TERM.

recent years among a population disturbed that some of its fellow citizens can still be born into privilege: "Royalty that celebrates its privileges in unsuitable company is living dangerously, but a monarch who clearly contributes to the development of society can bridge the gap between a culture of democracy and the right to inherit the throne." There are more than a passing similarity between the royals and Sweden's business elite. In a country where multiculturalism is celebrated and atheism is the norm, the white, patriarchal, Protestant and unelected institution at the pinnacle of society seems to stand for everything on which Sweden is trying to turn its back.

When, 20 years ago, leaders of Britain's centre-left Labour Party were trying to burnish their credentials with business, one of prime minister Tony Blair's leading ideologues famously said the party was "intensely relaxed about people getting filthy rich". There isn't a herring's chance in a pickling factory that any Swedish politician could get away with a statement like that, let alone somebody on the left. Sir Michael Marmot, leader of a seminal World Health Organization report on inequality and held up as something of a guru on the subject in Sweden, told me:

"In Sweden even right wing governments do not look so right wing, they broadly have the same commitment to a social democratic model."

All the same, Sweden has not been immune to international trends. There is an obvious tension between the country's traditional egalitarianism and its attempts to create an environment where capitalism, and capitalists, can flourish. So the rich have got richer in Sweden, as in many other countries. "There is a lot of rhetorical agreement on equality, very few politicians would say they are against it because we have such a strong egalitarian tradition here," says Per Molander, a former adviser to the IMF and author of a recent history of inequality. "But there is a large gap between rhetoric and reality. The fact is, the growth in inequality since the 1980s has been the largest among all OECD countries."

Sweden has long been seen as a paragon of fairness. The centre-left has governed the country for 80 of the past 100 years, for most of which it strived to be the folkhemmet – or people's home – in which the state was like a family, caring for all and with no one left behind. By all indicators, Sweden became one of the most socially equal countries in the world. A shift began when the Social Democrats began introducing free market policies and deregulating the credit market, but change accelerated after the 1990s economic crisis. "After that there was a sort of despair, a loss of control – the political energy to defend classical social democratic policies was simply not there any more," Molander says. A booming housing market and stock exchange led to soaring capital income from the sale of property and shares. Senior managers' income has "decoupled" from the rest, according to LO economist Thomas Carlén. Sweden now has nearly 200 krona billionaires, a number that has steadily increased over the past decade. Together, Sweden's richest own more than twice the annual budget of the Swedish state, and the number of dollar millionaires is also rising.

A fad among Stockholm's gilded youth in the years after the financial crash was vaskning – the ostentatious "sinking" of bottles of champagne by pouring them down the drain. Instead of buying one bottle you would get two, then ask the barman to pour one of them away. Meanwhile, in 2016 the UN children's agency Unicef reported that Sweden was on a "downward trajectory" in terms of the life chances for its poorest children, a growing number of whom were "very disadvantaged". A Swede with only a basic education can expect to live five years less than a university-educated compatriot, says the country's Public Health Agency. In my home town of Gothenburg, the gap between rich and poor almost quadrupled over two decades, according to a survey by the council. Its most shocking discovery was that people in affluent areas were living nine years longer than those in poor ones. When journalists compared a street of private mansions on the coast with overcrowded apartments occupied mainly by jobless immigrants on the other side of town, they found an income gap of more than half a million krona (€50,000).

By these measures, Sweden comes out clearly as a society of haves and have nots. However, when capital income is excluded, the gradual increase in inequality since the 1990s is significantly flatter – in other words, wages inequality has not grown so much. Where it has, the causes are fairly straightforward: tax cuts in some areas and cuts to welfare in others. Also, Sweden still ranks relatively high for social equality compared to other countries in Europe. Finally, the problem is recognised at a national level and there is growing political will to do something about it. Olle Lundberg, chair of the recently established Commission for Equity in Health, remarks that there has been a change in the political climate: "Now all the parties are talking about inequality," he says.

The three main cities, Stockholm, Gothenburg and Malmö, have set up organisations tasked with investigating the problem and what to do about it. The Equal Gothenburg programme is mobilising the city's resources and promising long-term investment to reduce inequalities, focusing in particular on children's early years. Political opposition to the programme is muted, more about how, rather than whether or why, to do something about it. The city's left-wing mayor, Ann-Sofie Hermansson, a former forklift driver at Volvo, told me:

"If you increase equality, you get more trust and stronger growth: it's a win-win situation. ... It is about decency, but it is also good for the economy."

Hermansson's suggestion that sustainable growth demands constraints on social inequalities is not a Gothenburg discovery, nor even a Swedish one. Some big hitters in the world economy have been pushing this message in recent years. The International Monetary Fund, which imposed free-market "stabilisation programmes" on wayward nations during the 1990s, argues to-day that reducing inequality can help support durable growth. Redistributive policies do not hamper but can even support growth, if appropriately de-signed, the IMF says. It goes so far as to suggest that increasing the income share of the poorest can boost an economy, while raising the income share of the richest can actually harm it. The IMF now says that all this puts address-ing inequality squarely within its mandate to help countries boost economic performance, and it is researching how countries can tax and spend dos effectively.

Research by another supranational body devoted to stimulating economic growth, the Organisation for Economic Cooperation and Development, has also found that reducing income inequality would boost economic growth, and that countries where income inequality is decreasing grow faster than those with rising inequality. "This compelling evidence proves that address-ing high and growing inequality is critical to promote strong and sustained growth and needs to be at the centre of the policy debate," said OECD secre-tary general Angel Gurría in 2014. "Countries that promote equal opportunity for all from an early age are those that will grow and prosper."

The OECD estimates that rising inequality knocked more than 10 percent-age points off growth in Mexico and New Zealand over the past two decades up to the global financial crash, while in Italy, the UK and the US the cumu-lative growth rate would have been six to nine percentage points higher had income disparities not widened. On the other hand, greater equality helped increase GDP per capita in Spain, France and Ireland prior to the crisis. The main mechanism through which inequality affects growth is by undermin-ing education opportunities for children from poor socio-economic back-grounds, lowering social mobility and hampering skills development, the OECD found. It also found no evidence that redistributive policies, such as taxes and welfare benefits, harm economic growth – provided, of course, that these policies are well designed and targeted.

So if Sweden can restore its sense of *lagom* in this sphere, and reverse its trend towards growing inequality, it will not just be reverting to historical type, but also singing in tune with recent economic thinking. Since social changes of this nature take time, they will demand far-sighted politicians looking to the long-term, rather than fixating on the next opinion poll. In this respect, the country's social policies would also be more in line with the investment approach of its biggest capitalists, which appear to pay more than lip service to long-term outcomes and recognise the need to spread the benefits of business throughout society.

SUMMARY CHAPTER 3

what more have we learned about our busy Swedish bumblebee?

• Swedish capitalists have a distinct attitude to the companies they own and control.

• This is partly because the country has a mechanism for hard-wiring a long-term approach into the way it runs its companies.

• That long-term approach hasn't stopped some Swedish companies from being extremely successful globally.

• Rather than an exclusive focus on short-term personal gain, this approach is also associated with a sense of wider responsibility for society.

• Some of Sweden's biggest capitalists believe that the market, and particularly the short-term share price, is only one measure of economic progress, and must be combined with others.

• None of this has prevented income inequality from rising rapidly in Sweden over the past 20 years.

• There is a broad political will to tackle rising inequality, because it is seen as damaging to society in the long run.

CHAPTER 4

ABSOLUTELY VABULOUS: WOMEN, WORK, AND THE FAMILY

Two women's experiences of having children abroad and in Sweden; how it all began with more rights for men; four decades of expanding childcare – and pushing men to take paternity leave; how it works for business; leading women reflect on the system's weaknesses

There it is: the thin blue line inside the window of the pregnancy test. After the initial elation, there is a nagging question: how are we going to afford the childcare? I think it is probably fair to say that this is a sensation unknown to most Swedes. It is no secret that, in relative terms, Swedish parents enjoy significant paid time off work to be with small children, while daycare facilities are heavily subsidised by the state. There might be many questions about how a child will change the way you live your life, but "Can we pay for childcare?" is not one of them.

"This is one of the things that you take for granted when you are born in Sweden. It is amazing, it gives you freedom," says Linnéa Mitchell, a yoga instructor in Stockholm. She gave birth to Theo in London in 2010, and to Freja in Stockholm four years later, so has experienced the contrast between having a child at home and abroad. When Theo came along, Mitchell had already quit her London job. Before the birth, her experience of the taxpayer-funded UK National Health Service was very good, and for 18 months Mitchell was happy to be at home with her son – her British husband Phil was on good money. But it was when she wanted to get back into work that the problems

began. Soon the family was paying the equivalent of €400 a month for Theo to spend just three mornings a week at a kindergarten.

"It was then I realised it was financially not viable to go back to work," Mitchell recalls. "I would have had to earn a lot to pay for childcare and have anything left." In London she had a circle of women friends with small children, most of whom were keen to get back to the workplace. But with the man earning more in most cases, it ended up being the woman who took on the domestic role. Others found they had to go back part time. "They were educated and accustomed to feeling valued at work, and all of a sudden here they were chatting to other mums on the school run," Mitchell says. "I wanted to be independent and earn my own income, but we longed for another child. I refused to have another baby as long as we stayed in London – I just couldn't do it, I needed more support. It became psychological – what was my worth, what was the point of my going back to work? There was pressure for Phil to earn big bucks. In the end we were convinced we had to move to Sweden if we wanted another child."

Back in Stockholm, Mitchell called the social services. They asked when Theo was born – and handed the couple 480 days paid time off work, to be used before he reached the age of 8. The authorities made an estimate of Mitchell's earnings if had she been employed, using it calculate the money she would receive. "It is so easy, you just fill in your details," she explains, looking back. "You don't have to do anything, everything is taken care of for you." She found a kindergarten, or *dagis*, near their apartment that would take Theo any time between 8am and 5pm, five days a week – for around €100 a month. "It was completely different story from London, such a contrast," she says. "I struggled mentally with our first child, because I was so used to taking control of my own life. London and Stockholm were like night and day. If I mention all this to Americans their heads just explode!"

Daughter Freja came along a year after the Mitchells moved to Sweden. There was another difference: no one raised an eyebrow if she or her husband left work early to pick up a sick child. "What would we do without VAB? It is fabulous," she says. VAB stands for *vård av barn*, or care for the child. VAB means parents can take up to 120 paid days off work a year to be with a sick child aged up to age 12.

Women who have read this far, or perhaps have chosen to open this book at this very chapter, may have mixed feelings about reading further. Young women in most of Europe, Asia and North America will be inspired by the Swedish example, but they can also expect to feel frustrated – the reality they will face when they come to give birth in their home countries is likely to be very different from the picture outlined here. Women who have already been through this difficult period in their lives might feel regret: so this is what it could have been like? What if the father and I had had these opportunities? How different could our lives have been, and those of our children? Sweden's system of extended parental leave, heavily subsidised kindergartens, and generous time off to be with sick children is certainly no panacea. Having a family is hard work, physically and emotionally, and particularly for the woman. But in terms of support for working parents and families, Sweden is way out in front compared to most of the globe.

From the point of view of this book, Sweden's tax-and-spend approach to raising the next generation seems to be the part of the bumblebee's anatomy most likely to hobble its flight – as if the legs were so laden with pollen that it couldn't possibly get off the ground. But family policy also opens a fresh, more modern and political perspective on the Swedish model. The country is increasingly identified internationally with the way it champions women's rights; for Swedes themselves who travel or work abroad, the childcare system at home stands out, making them feel distinct from other nations on a level beyond blond hair and Abba.

101

"Swedes are aware that we are different in this respect," says Ann-Zofie Duvander, a sociology professor at Stockholm University who specialises in family policy. "There is conscious idea that Swedish family policy is generous and we are different. In interviews, parents state that they know they are lucky." When I got together with my future wife Annika in London in 2011, she wanted to go home to have babies. Many Swedish women living abroad feel the call of home most strongly when they think about starting a family. "They have really dreadful childcare in Switzerland," says a mother on an internet forum discussing the situation for Swedish women abroad. "It is shit expensive in Canada, and there is no VAB," says another. "No VAB in Spain either," says a third. "Due to childcare costs in the UK, and the lack of VAB, it is still very common for one of the parents not to work – mostly the mother," says a fourth. "There doesn't appear to be a country that can compare with Swedish parental benefits. It's a jungle out there."

Hannah Raffelsberger is a New Zealander who has worked all over the world. She fell pregnant with her first child in San Francisco, which turned out to be the beginning of the end of her life in the USA. "It cost $5,000 to give birth in hospital, but I was insured," she says. "But the company I worked for wouldn't give me any paid days off after having my child. That was a deal breaker, the end of my working career in the States." American friends told her stories about having to save up to stay at home with a baby, and day care

"THE WHOLE MENTALITY IS THAT CHILDREN WHO COME FROM LESS FORTUNATE BACKGROUNDS SHOULD HAVE THE SAME EXPERIENCES AS OTHERS. I THINK THAT IS FANTASTIC – IT'S NOT THEIR FAULT THAT THEY WERE BORN INTO A PARTICULAR FAMILY. THESE ARE GREAT VALUES THAT SWEDEN HAS."

Hannah Raffelsberger, *international business development manager at Arla Plast*

being "crazy expensive". So she quit the job and moved to Austria, where her husband was at medical school. Later the family moved to New Zealand, where Raffelsberger worked full time. Things were a little easier than the US, but still very tough. Soon she was spending a "huge chunk" of her salary on daycare, or about NZ$500 (€350) a week. "You start asking yourself: apart from your mental health, what is the benefit of going to work? You are just working to live," she says.

In New Zealand, Raffelsberger could take just five paid sick days a year, regardless of whether it was for herself or to look after her child. She and husband Jens, who has joint Swedish-Austrian citizenship, moved to Sweden in 2004 when their eldest was 3 years and their daughter was 2 months old. "We were not aware of the rights we had, so we were muddled and found out things along the way," she recalls. "Social services announced that we were eligible for a retrospective payment – two whole years of child allowance. Jens and I looked at each other and said: wow!" Child allowance was worth about €100 a month. The couple had a third child, and both parents were able to stay home for several months. "When the children were small they went to day care, it was so nice, they made me feel good about dropping the children off," she says.

The Raffelsbergers then spent some years away from Sweden, returning in 2014 to settle in a small town in the south. This time Hannah appreciated the flexibility for working mothers – she had the right to work part-time if she wanted, varying the hours to suit the family. Her youngest would finish school at 1:30 pm, but could have after-school activities until 5 or 6 o'clock. The children could also sign up for low-cost sports programs. At no cost, her 15-year-old daughter was fitted with braces for her teeth; in New Zealand it would have cost NZ$10,000. Raffelsberger says:

"Swedes are definitely pro family and pro developing the young human being to a fuller extent. The whole mentality is that children that come from less fortunate backgrounds should have the same experiences as others. I think that is fantastic – it's not their fault that they were born into a particular economic background. These are great values that Sweden has."

Since the foundation's of Sweden's childcare provision were laid in the 1970s, the system has expanded enormously. But rather than simply drool over how wonderful it all is, this chapter will look at how childcare has gone from an economic necessity to becoming part of Sweden's self-identity. We will also look at the problems it causes, the costs involved, and the mountain still to climb in terms of women's rights.

'SEX DISCRIMINATION IS WASTEFUL'

It all began with more rights for men. In 1974 Sweden became the world's first nation to explicitly allow fathers to take paid time off from work to look after a small child. This reform meant that couples could share six months of parental leave, on 90% of their pay, over the first eight years of the child's life. Mothers already had this right, but sharing it with fathers was a big step in a sustained campaign to usher more women into the workforce by encouraging employment before childbirth, with the right to return to their former workplace after maternity leave. There were few who expected significant numbers of fathers to take up the offer of sharing childcare, but this was still a landmark – for the first time, a national government had acknowledged that parenthood and nursing work were not just for women, but also for men.

Putting the case for men to do more childcare, Olof Palme, the enigmatic left-wing aristocrat who led the country at the time, described the outcome of the debate within Swedish society that led to this reform: "In order that women shall be emancipated from their antiquated role, the men must also be emancipated. ... The aim over the long run must be that men and women should be given the same rights, obligations and work assignments in society. This fundamental idea is today embraced by almost all political parties in Sweden." However, as Palme also admitted, this way of thinking was "still in a strident contrast to the factual conditions".

Before these changes were set in motion, Swedish women had been largely viewed as housewives and mothers, and treated as such; in the 1950s, Sweden had a lower participation rate of women in the workforce than Britain. However, from the 1960s, Swedish women were encouraged to take jobs to meet Sweden's acute postwar labour shortage. With this evolution came an insight that an altered role for women required changes in the role of men. Slogans about the positive consequences for fathers of sharing domestic tasks were just a start. "We have to expand society's facilities for childcare," Palme said. "When women as well as men go out to work, society has to be organised accordingly. This is vital in order to provide children with a stimulating and diversified environment in which to grow. It fortifies women's ambitions to achieve equality in working life."

105

With the die cast, and Swedish politicians and businesses largely united in favour of both parents going to work, there was a pressing need to expand provision of childcare outside the home to meet the needs of working couples. Female participation in the economy grew steadily – by the early-1990s women constituted nearly half the Swedish labour force, the highest percentage anywhere in the world. The blue-collar trade union federation LO became a leading advocate for public childcare, as its women members demanded support. The union's calls complemented the agenda of business and the state to foster an environment where women could work outside the home while still having children, thereby aiming for full employment alongside relatively high fertility rates. The number of publicly provided childcare places increased rapidly, from under 12,000 in 1965 to over 136,000 by 1980. Simultaneously, the amount of paid time off for parents grew to nine months in 1978, 12 months in 1980, and 15 months in 1989.

Yet men stubbornly refused to take up the chance to spend time with their children. In the scheme's first year men took only 0.5 per cent of all paid parental leave. The centre-right government that kicked out Palme in 1976 launched an advertising campaign featuring Swedish weightlifter Lennart Dahlgren, nicknamed "Hoa-Hoa" for his habit of roaring himself into a frenzy before a lift. With his mane of red hair, Dahlgren was depicted cradling a baby on his biceps in a national poster campaign to encourage men to take paternity leave. It had little or no impact. When the right came to power again in 1991, in the midst of a severe economic slump, the number of fathers taking paternity leave had stalled at 6 per cent.

But this crisis government was not just concerned with the immediate problems of a banking collapse. For Bengt Westerberg, the Liberal Party leader who was now minister for social affairs in a very pro-business government, this was an opportunity to tackle a problem that had long concerned him – gender inequality and men's non-existent role in childcare. During the 1980s, Westerberg had railed against the effects of discrimination against women. "The lack of gender equality is not only an injustice against the women and men who suffer, it also means failing to make use of human resources," he told Sweden's parliament. For Westerberg, a middle-aged civil servant whose parents ran the family paint shop south of Stockholm, inequality was about economic inefficiency. "Gender discrimination and rigid thinking are wasteful. Especially in times of financial difficulties, we need to use each person's individuality, initiative, and willingness to take responsibility. Women have a lot to offer the labour market, business and politics. Men have a lot to offer and are needed for work in the home and with children."

Westerberg now set out to raise the number of men taking paternity leave. Following intense political debate, the government decided to force men to take at least a month of paternity leave. This "daddy month" reserved for fathers became law in 1995. Sweden was not the first – Norway had taken a similar step two years earlier. "I always thought if we made it easier for women to work, families would eventually choose a more equal division of parental leave by themselves," Westerberg told the New York Times some years later. "But I gradually became convinced that there wasn't all that much choice. ... Society is a mirror of the family. The only way to achieve equality in society is to achieve equality in the home. Getting fathers to share the parental leave is an essential part of that."

The new law making paternity leave compulsory had an immediate impact. A new Child Care Act obliged city councils to provide care for children aged 12 months and upwards "without unreasonable delay". Stockholm also placed a cap on what councils could charge, making the system even more affordable. Subsidised childcare places expanded to nearly 730,000 by 2002. So despite the economic crisis of the early 1990s, Sweden still managed to expand its system of childcare dramatically, at a time when it was cutting back on other aspects of the welfare state.

The young men with a few days stubble whom you see around town pushing their buggies to the nearest cafe are known as "latte pappas". Today, fathers take around a quarter of the total parental leave on average; one in 10 couples divide it 40:60 between father and mother, which is twice as many as in the 1990s. In 2002, a second month of compulsory paternity leave was introduced; debate over the measure was muted this time because the principle had already been established. A third "daddy month" was added in 2016. Men also use about a third of the available days off for VAB – those 120 paid days per year off to be with a sick child.

Expectations have changed, with more women assuming that their partner will share the childcare, and more companies relaxed about male workers disappearing to have kids (see below). Indeed, some businesses top up employees' income when they take parental leave, after earnings compensation was trimmed during the 1990s recession. Nationally, Sweden spends four times as much of its wealth on early childhood education and care than the United States, or around 1.6 per cent of its GDP. About half of this goes on the cost of paid parental leave. In total, parents pay slightly more than 10 per cent of the gross costs of childcare, with the state and the municipalities covering the lion's share. The law states that families should never pay more than 4 per cent of their income on childcare.

So where does this leave the Swedish model and its various bumblebee features? For almost half a century the country has been out in front in terms of subsidised childcare and paid time off for parents with small children. It has taken several bold initiatives, each of which has demanded years of debate and preparation. The driving forces have been both economic, as Sweden sought to maximise the potential of its indigenous workforce, and political, as social democratic and liberal politicians pursued an ideal of equality between men and women as a goal in itself. In consequence, the system for enabling women to combine work and children looks similar today to how it was in 1974 – just bigger and better.

The private sector was allowed to enter the childcare market a generation ago, but three-quarters of kindergartens are still municipal services, and most of the "freestanding" ones are provided by employee and parent cooperatives. Private, for-profit childcare has not expanded much beyond the wealthy suburbs of Stockholm, in contrast to elderly care, for example, where services have become less universal and more selective. All childcare facilities are tightly controlled and regulated by councils and the state. So it is in the family sphere that the traditional Swedish welfare state is strongest, still adhering to the values of social equality and fair distribution of life chances that it was born with in the 1970s. While most rich nations have seen an expansion of family policy in recent decades, Sweden sticks out

Hannah Raffelsberger with her children and husband Jens. And the dog, of course. Expectations in Sweden are changing – more women assume their partner will share the childcare, and more companies are relaxed about men taking time off to do so.

as a consistent champion of feminism and gender equality, says Kenneth Nelson, professor of comparative social policy at Stockholm University:

"The family is the area that stands out as being pretty much unique – in other areas, Sweden is moving relatively closer to the liberal welfare state as in the UK and US. Family policy, parental leave and childcare have not suffered from substantial cutbacks, rather the opposite, they have expanded even further. In Sweden these policies are not such a politically contested issue. Even the economists think it's a good thing, not least in terms of increasing the labour force and employment – you make it possible for two-earner households, it's good for the economy as a whole. That's one of the major reasons these policies have been unaffected."

There is remarkable political unity over family policy. The small Christian Democrat party has campaigned for more "choice" for parents to decide how to raise their children, proposing a care allowance that would make it possible for parents of young children to stay at home longer than the time allotted by the parental leave system, or to employ a domestic nanny instead of using public childcare. But the low take-up of such a scheme after 2008 meant it was later scrapped. The far-right Sweden Democrats, who are a more significant force in Swedish politics, are hostile to feminism, but they are even more hostile towards Islam. The party has increasingly used an argument that gender equality is a feature of Swedish culture as a means of focusing on differences between Swedes and Muslims, and emphasising women's oppression by Islam. The party says words to the effect that "Muslims don't like women, they are threatening our Swedish way of life".

For these reasons, one of the architects of Sweden's recovery from its 1990s economic woes has a point when he identifies family policy as integral to the Swedish model. "We have chosen to go for these family friendly programmes and they have worked," says Göran Persson, the Social Democratic prime minister from 1996 to 2006. "Parental leave is rational. Sweden makes it possible to combine a professional career with the responsibility for two or three kids." Persson points to the universities: if female students feel they have to choose between becoming a mother or a professional, many would opt to be professionals, de-prioritising family life:

"And if that happens, a society without children will end up in a very difficult situation. The 66-year-old is not a driving force for economic growth, it is the 6-year-old. In a society dominated by 6-year-olds you are forced to discuss climate change and so on, because you are future-oriented. Older people look back and ask why did this not happen, whose fault is it, who should I blame? Look at Trump voters in the US. But where kids are at the centre, we are forced to discuss the future. That is also why family policy is part of the Swedish model."

For some, this is evidence of a "new" Swedish model, one that has moved away from an economic focus on relations between trade unions and employers towards a close association with feminist values. "The old Swedish model was the compromise with labour, but the new model is gender equality, it is more ideological," says Henrik Berggren, biographer of Olof Palme. This is Palme's legacy, he says, rather than his left-wing posturing on issues such as the Vietnam war, which gave him such a reputation as an internationalist firebrand. The approach has solid roots in society, rather than being an expression of identity politics or Sweden's more recent grandstanding on

111

"THE OLD SWEDISH MODEL WAS THE COMPROMISE WITH LABOUR, BUT THE NEW MODEL IS GENDER EQUALITY, IT IS MORE IDEOLOGICAL."

Henrik Berggren, *biographer of Olof Palme*

human rights. In some ways, Berggen says, Palme was continuing a conservative Swedish tradition that celebrates family values and seeks to strengthen them. "The Social Democrats have been most successful as a national egalitarian project. Palme's Swedish model was parental leave, which he put in place in the 1970s. The ground that the conservatives stand on today is just that – a gender model where you talk about equality of the sexes."

'A LONG WAY TO GO'

For Ronnie Leten, the Belgian chairman of Swedish corporation Ericsson, Swedish parental leave policies came as a shock. He first moved to Sweden from Antwerp in 2009 to become the head of tool-maker Atlas Copco. He recalls his surprise when faced with the length of a woman's maternity leave: "My attitude was: Oh my God! She should come back after 10 or 18 weeks. I can't cope with it, put the child in day care!"

Over the next seven years he changed his mind. "There is a difference between long illness and parental leave," he says, speaking in late 2016. "Parenthood is a planned absence. You have six months early warning once she is pregnant, so you can plan it." There are also positive aspects, he says. Rather than just the need to fill a vacancy, this can be a valuable opportunity to rotate talent in the company and try out other people in that job. The people who come forward show themselves as open to challenges and willing to try something new. "People who step in know it is temporary, so you find a market for people who are willing to do that. You find people motivated to do it, and most likely who will bring something new. And after 12 months there are no emotions – they know the guy is coming back."

Leten was forced to look again at what employees need to stay motivated over the longer term. The ideal from the company point of view is to keep the whole team together, "working their butts off and having fun", he says. "But is that sustainable? You need to have relaxation time, a balance between private life and work." It was his son, who had two small kids, who opened Leten's eyes to the pressures faced by families in which both parents work. Now, his attitude to parental leave in Sweden has undergone a transformation:

"I would not even call it generous – they give young couples a very respect-ful gift from society. This little boy or girl is your responsibility to grow it up in a warm nest and make sure it becomes a fantastic contributor to society. Putting them in daycare after 10 weeks – is that really the sort of society we want? That's how I see we should interpret it."

This sounds like the same long-term view of business, and of the wider loy-alties of businesspeople to society, that we encountered in Chapter 3. In the same vein, Tom Johnstone, a Scott and a board member for several Swedish corporations, has a neat response to those who doubt the benefits of gener-ous parental leave: "Obviously it doesn't damage business because otherwise you wouldn't have so many successful businesses here," he says. "There is a cost to it – you just have to manage it." Like Leten, Johnstone takes the broader view: "The bond formed between parents and baby early on is so important. Here in Sweden we focus much more on wellbeing and equality – and I truly feel we get the benefit in business."

Hans Enocson, former CEO of GE in Sweden, says something similar about women taking long periods of maternity leave: "I feel the challenge, but it is worthwhile. I believe in a society where you can be a balanced individual. My colleagues in different parts of the world find it very strange: in Germany it is part of the culture for women to stay home, while in the US maternity leave is a few weeks. What counts is productivity, loyalty, having people who enjoy working for the company. And then they pay you back." Whatever happens to parents is not something employers have to worry about – the systems are in place, all arranged by the government. Sorted.

This is a politically correct point of view, and managers are wary of courting controversy on this issue. "It is a forbidden topic, you have to behave properly," says Håkan Mogren, a director of the Wallenberg investment company Investor. "It is impossible to cut maternity leave because it is taken for granted. I never touch this subject because it is so hot." In fact there is evidence that favourable attitudes among top bosses reflect a more general shift of opinion in economic circles. Philip Hwang, a psychology professor at Gothenburg University, has been surveying companies' attitudes since 1993. In 2009, he and his American colleague Linda Haas reported "dramatic improvement" in corporate support within large Swedish companies for fathers taking leave, measured in terms of formal policies, informal support from co-workers and managers, and the observation that periods of paternity leave become the norm. The biggest change was the introduction of formal paternity leave policies, which were now in place at more than four out of 10 companies.

"Swedish parental leave policy," the researchers concluded, "appears to have been successful in reducing corporate resistance toward fathers taking leave, helping to make fatherhood more visible at work." Employer's attitudes were an important factor in fathers taking less time off with kids, as were other dads in the workplace doing so, or working in women-dominated workplaces. The public sector was friendlier towards fathers than the private sector, and there was a class aspect: fathers used more parental allowance if their income was high.

But the researchers also found that family friendly policies are still regarded as more of a benefit for women than men, because the belief has lingered that this is a natural role to which women are better suited. "The male norm of full-time employment remains strong even in Sweden," Hwang said in 2016. Fewer than half of mothers go back to work full-time after having a baby, while almost all men work full-time after paternity leave. Generous family support has increased the number of working women, but much of that has been in part-time work; for example, half the women members of the LO trade union federation are part time.

Meanwhile, women are less likely to be in management and professional occupations. Swedish women experience a large drop in relative earnings following the birth of their first child, and the gap is larger in the top jobs, consistent with the idea of a "glass ceiling" that limits women from moving up the organisation. Extended absence of someone in a top job is particularly expensive, so companies tend to place relatively few women in fast-track career positions. Women, even those who would otherwise be strongly career-oriented, understand that their promotion possibilities are limited and may respond by choosing more family-friendly jobs and careers – and by taking more parental leave than their partners. As a result, gender segregation

"PARENTAL LEAVE IS HOLY, HOW CAN YOU ATTACK IT? BUT TIME
OFF SHOULD BE SHARED EQUALLY BETWEEN MEN AND WOMEN.
OTHERWISE IT HOLDS WOMEN BACK."

Karin Forseke, *former chief executive of Swedish investment bank Carnegie*

in the economy becomes a self-fulfilling prophecy because of the the behaviour of employers and workers alike. There is therefore a strong argument
that, so long as family responsibilities are unequally shared, the gender gap is
not likely to narrow significantly, even in a highly flexible labour market such
as Sweden's.

Interviews for this book suggested that women at the top of Swedish industry seem to be more aware of limits to the system than their male counterparts, and more conscious of informal patterns of put-downs, condescen-
sion, and downright discrimination in the workplace that still exist, despite
the right-on policies and rhetoric. "In most families, the husband drops the
children off in the morning and the mothers pick them up – that's an issue
for women in the workforce," says Karin Forseke, former chief executive of
Swedish investment bank Carnegie, when she was one of very few female
bosses of companies listed on the Stockholm Stock Exchange. She says:

*"Women will leave at 3pm or 4pm to collect the kids, but the fathers can
work late and go out for a beer after work. Today it is still the women who
carry the greatest burden. There are unconscious biases and stereotypical
behaviour, this is still a patriarchal society. We have made great progress
but we have a long way to go."*

Forseke says she felt more valued when she worked in the United States, where she found success was measured in results, regardless of race or gender. Swedes hide behind the slogans of the Swedish model, Forseke says, preferring to believe that things are "the best in the world" instead of looking below the surface. "We should have a more open and frank discussion, but we are very afraid of that," she says. "Every system has its strengths and weaknesses and other parts of the world do certain things better. Parental leave is holy, how can you attack it? But time off should be shared equally between men and women. Otherwise it holds women back."

Anna Bråkenhielm, a serial entrepreneur who established the organisation Passion for Business to help women reach the top, is "not a huge fan" of long maternity leave, because it means women lose time when they could be developing their careers. She wrote her first newspaper column about the issue in 2002, since when the number of women in top jobs has changed by only a few percent. Sweden is too liberal in allowing families to decided who should stay at home with the baby, she argues — parental leave should be divided equally between mother and father:

118

"If you look at who owns companies and wealth it is men; women are not willing to risk or sacrifice their personal lives and families. If you are a business person and a man you are excused from looking after the home. As a man you won't have a bad conscience about being away from your family; as a woman you always have to say sorry. I have stopped doing that with my teenage kids now – I talk to them about how much I enjoy my work and travelling. I want them to see me happy in my job. My mother, a doctor and politician, always complained about the burden of work, but I knew deep down that she loved her jobs but didn't want to admit it. Things are changing in the right direction, but very slowly."

Bråkenhielm points to the 2015 scandal that shook Sweden's corporate elite after journalists lifted the lid on a culture of lavish perks and extravagance, in which wives, children and even top executives' pets were flown in corporate jets to a luxury hunting lodge, Formula One races, the football World Cup and the Olympics. The people involved often sat on the boards of each other's companies, and even okayed each other's expenses. The scandal was widely reported as evidence of a closed and incestuous world in which executives lived by different rules to the rest of us. But Bråkenhielm says it was also proof of the overwhelming dominance of men in the corridors of corporate power. "The scandal shows that it was a male bastion, a closed structure with no women, the same guys all the time," she says.

One Swedish woman to make it to the top in a very masculine environment is Petra Einarsson, the first female chief executive of high-tech steel maker Sandvik Materials Technology (SMT), and now CEO of BillerudKorsnäs, a maker of sustainable packaging. Starting at SMT as a trainee after leaving university in 1989, she worked her way up to become Sweden's most powerful business woman with her appointment as CEO in 2013. She sees herself as a role model, but she is acutely aware that just being female in a top job is not enough, and she is frustrated at the slow pace of change. "If I hadn't been affected by living for 25 years in a totally male dominated organisation there would be something wrong with me," she says wryly in SMT's low-ceilinged offices on Kungsbron, central Stockholm. "I see every day how women are treated differently from men. But if you start to get totally frustrated and angry, it becomes difficult to change it." Instead, her tactic is to stay calm and challenge men's behaviour:

"YOU COULD HAVE MORE IMPACT ON THE WORLD THAN IF YOU BECOME A DOCTOR ... CLEAN WATER, SAFE NUCLEAR PLANTS, LOWER CARBON EMISSIONS – THEY ALL DEMAND TECHNOLOGICAL SHIFTS. BUT WE HAVE TO HAVE THE GUTS IN THE INDUSTRY TO SAY THAT."

Petra Einarsson, *chief executive of BillerudKorsnäs*

120

"The thing is not to make the guys look ridiculous. The men who treat women differently to the way they treat men don't do so to be mean or because they are bad people, but because they are accustomed to doing it. If you hold up a mirror to them, they always say: 'Really? Oh no, I don't want to be like that.' If you challenge a man, they will see their attitudes and behaviour, and so change is possible. Then you have contributed by helping men to see. That is my tactic to cope with it, rather than internalising it and complaining afterwards: 'Did you see what happened in that meeting?'"

Getting more women interested in technology means making them feel welcome and talking about what companies like hers can do – that they are not all about machines, and if you come to Sandvik you can make a positive difference. "We are creating sustainable technologies that will change the world; here you could have more impact on the world than if you become a doctor," Einarsson says. "Clean water, safe nuclear plants, lower carbon emissions – they all demand technological shifts. But we have to have the guts in the industry to say that."

As the first female boss in Sandvik's 150-year history, Einarsson feels the under-representation of women at the top of business is a "failure" for Sweden. Women's situation has improved – men taking time off with children is a huge change from not being home at all. "So there is hope for the future," she says. "But gender diversity is taking too long, it is such a struggle. Sometimes I think: I am a woman, I am in charge, I should just fix it. But it is not so easy."

Petra Einarsson, one of the few women in a top position in engineering:

"Gender diversity is taking too long, it is such a struggle to increase the numbers.

Sometimes I think: I am a woman, I am in charge. Just fix it! But it is not so easy."

SUMMARY CHAPTER 4

What has this chapter taught us about our gender-conscious Swedish bumblebee?

- The Swedish system of generous parental leave and subsidised childcare is no panacea, but it's very good

- This includes 120 paid days off a year to care for sick children, known as VAB

- The system has its political roots in a leftist government of the 1970s, but both liberal and conservative governments have pushed for its expansion

124

- It was a liberal politician in the 1990s who first forced Swedish men to take paternity leave

- It is in the family sphere that the traditional, state-run Swedish welfare system is strongest today

- The system originated in a shortage of workers and the need for women to fill the gap, but a political commitment to gender equality has become an integral aspect

- Business attitudes to lengthy parental leave tend to mirror the long-term outlook that we encountered in Chapter 3

- There are signs that corporate reluctance for fathers to take paternity leave is weakening

- Women in the workplace still have to battle against stereotypes and discrimination

- There is evidence of a "glass ceiling", higher than which women find it hard to climb

CHAPTER 5

'OUR SYSTEM IS BEING TESTED': THE CHALLENGE OF IMMIGRATION

The Stockholm riots of 2013; the great wave of asylum seekers; getting refugees into jobs; the debate over low wages; solving the housing shortage and segregation; Sweden's big immigration debate

A smell of burning tyres mingled with the scent of cherry blossom that grew so thick it seemed every tree was detonating in a soft, pink explosion. This was May 2013, and I had just set foot in Stockholm. The short nights of early summer meant there were still several hours of daylight ahead when I dropped my bags and walked up the hill into Husby. This small suburb was making international headlines because its youth was in revolt, torching cars and fighting with the police. When I got the call, I was sitting in a dull conference on corporate governance, in a village on the west coast. It was all kicking off in Stockholm, but the *Financial Times* correspondent for the region, who has been itching to cover a big political story like this, had just boarded the slow boat to Legoland in Denmark with his son. This made me the FT journalist nearest to the story. I didn't need to be asked twice to get myself to the capital.

It seemed like an unlikely place for a riot. The walkways between the apartment blocks were quiet, lined with well-kept verge and rhododendrons. At the top of the hill I entered a setting I would see again and again in Swedish suburbs after I immigrated permanently a few months later – a narrow, drab pedestrian area, lined by a few single-storey shops clad in grey concrete. But tonight it was full of people. Black and brown people. Mainly men, of all ages,

some dressed in the flowing tunics and baggy trousers of their original home-lands. Nobody paid me the slightest attention – there were serious things afoot. I adopted a tactic that has since stood me in good stead, proffering a big smile and asking: "Do you speak English?" For two days and nights I tramped happily around Husby, talking to anyone and everyone, notebook in hand, a somewhat exotic figure for the locals. A Tunisian called Abdul took me under his wing and helped me to eavesdrop on conversations.

The crowds I met on that first night were not rioting – they were out to try and stop the rioters, remonstrating with the young men who were throwing stones, burning cars and trashing schools. For that brief week in May, the cup of discontent ran over among Sweden's immigrant youth, who drew the world's attention to their grievances in the only way they knew how. A sense of in-justice had been building for years. Husby felt like a ghetto, with sub-standard housing and people trapped on welfare, unable to get jobs. Facilities for young people had closed down, schools were overcrowded and underfunded. This is the story of immigrant Sweden. Every large town has one or more areas like this, where you cross the road and suddenly every face is dark-skinned. Today the share of the population with a foreign background in Husby is more than 70 per cent, predominantly from Africa and the Arab world. In neighbouring Rinkeby, which became notorious a few years later for shootings and gang violence, it is 90 per cent.

The rioters were second generation youth, born in Sweden, speaking Swed-ish like the natives and feeling themselves to be Swedes. All repeated the same story – they were treated as second class citizens by white Swedish society. Behind this lay a broader grievance about racism. Yunis, from Yemen, had kept his teenage son at home that week. He had high hopes for his star pupil, but feared that attitudes would make it hard for him to get work. "Maybe I should change his name," Yunis said. "They see Ali or Abdul or whatever, and that's it, suddenly there is no job."

The intensity of the 2013 unrest shocked the world. France and Britain had experienced riots in recent years, but Sweden was supposed to be different. How could a high-wage, high-welfare society coexist alongside pockets of deprivation? How could the country's leaders claim to represent a "humanitar-ian superpower" – spending proportionately more of the nation's income on foreign aid than any other country in 2015 – at the same time as they presided over extreme levels of segregation and inequality at home?

Furthermore, this was the year in which the great refugee exodus to Europe from the war-torn Middle East and Africa was gathering momentum. At its peak two years later, Sweden received more than 160,000 asylum seekers, the highest number per capita after Hungary, which took far fewer than Sweden in the preceding years as the crisis began. In the five years to 2016 – after which numbers dropped sharply – Sweden received 370,000 asylum seekers, or 3.5 per cent of its total population. According to the official figures, more than half of these – including relatives who came to join them – were granted temporary or indefinite permission to remain. Could the model absorb these large numbers of people, find them jobs, somewhere to live, schools for their children, and turn them into productive contributors to society?

At first, political leaders expressed a soaring humanitarianism that seemed to border on the naive. Prime minister Fredrik Reinfeldt, leader of Sweden's Conservative centre-right, urged Swedes to "open their hearts" to refugees. Some felt he was asking them to "open their wallets", with taxpayers subsidising the liberal elite's multiculturalist fantasies. Having lost the election, Reinfeldt defended himself: "I often fly across the Swedish countryside and I would advise more people to do that," he said. "There are endless fields and forests. There is more space than you can imagine. Those who claim that the country is full, they should show us where it is full." Was the former prime minister really suggesting that Sweden's size alone meant it could cope with unlimited immigration at a whirlwind pace? It presented the anti-immigrant Sweden Democrats party with an open goal. New arrivals needed infrastructure, housing, schools and healthcare, they said.

A year later, a thousand asylum seekers were crossing into the country every day from Denmark, drawn by tales of Swedish generosity and understanding. Turning out to welcome them, the centre-left prime minister Stefan Löfven told a crowd of Stockholmers that his vision of Europe was one that receives people fleeing from war: "My Europe does not build walls, we help when the need is great." What seemed like a tough job would, in the long run, be an asset for Sweden, he said. This attitude, an embodiment of Reinfeldt's "open your hearts", lasted about two months, to be replaced by nothing short of panic. In November the government slammed the door shut and imposed tough measures to deter asylum seekers. "It pains me that Sweden is no longer capable of receiving asylum seekers at the high level we do today. We simply cannot do it any more," Löfven announced. His deputy burst into tears. "The last bastion of humanitarianism has fallen," a United Nations official told me. Refugee arrivals in Sweden plummeted overnight.

But now that they were here, what was Sweden going to do with them? On the European and North American right, a narrative emerged – large-scale immigration was a disaster and Sweden would be punished for its generosity with rising crime and violence. The country was set up as a whipping boy for multiculturalism, a deterrent to any moves to allow more migrants into Europe and the United States. This account went viral in February 2017, when the newly elected US president, Donald Trump, claimed that a terror attack had taken place "last night in Sweden", when the night in question had in fact been entirely peaceful. Now the anti-immigrant right set out to prove that Trump was onto something after all, and that Sweden was a country over-run by dark-skinned criminals, rapists, murderers and terrorists. Social media was inundated by allegations of this nature, a prophecy that seemed fulfilled in April when Rakhmat Akilov, a 39-year-old asylum seeker from Uzbekistan, drove a truck into pedestrians on Stockholm's main shopping street, killing five in the name of Islamic State. Sweden's immigrant areas were now "no go zones", the right claimed – a distortion that has become a meme. In a spiral of rhetoric, Swedish officials began referring to "war zones"; there was talk of sending in the army.

I have wandered around many of these "no go areas" during my time in Sweden, meeting some remarkable people in the process. This has included turning up at the site of a machine-gun gang attack, and visiting an area after a crazed young racist went on the rampage, slashing immigrants with a Samurai sword. Only on one occasion have I felt unsafe, and that was because of my own foolishness. I was in Rosengård, an infamous estate in Malmö, during a spate of grenade attacks in the city. Before sitting with young people among the apartment blocks, I visited the police station, but one of the locals saw me come out. "He's a cop," he said, and the atmosphere turned frosty. To win back some trust I agreed to puff on a joint that was being handed around. Man, that was some strong shit. With my tongue stuck to the roof of my mouth and my short-term memory shot to pieces, I attempted to interview these guys, getting answers to questions that I couldn't even remember asking. Never again.

For this book, I went back to Husby in January 2018. "We too can dream big!" said a freshly painted slogan outside the small community centre. But several shops had closed down, including a supermarket, shuttered for more than a year. Young people were smoking cannabis in the stairwells. The library was closed that day because of staff shortages, disappointing a string of young mothers with small children. A new block of flats had just been completed, but the corrugated cladding on the other blocks was stained and shabby. Young black people were notably more suspicious of me than five years previously. "What's your agenda?" they asked, and complained that nothing had changed. The hairdresser, an Iranian in her 50s, was struggling to keep her business afloat; the politicians were to blame, she said. But at least Husby had calmed down, there was no more rioting or arson. Abdullah, an asylum seeker from Iraq, pointed above his head to a ball of mirror glass – security cameras had

> "We too can dream big!" – slogan outside Husby's community centre.

been installed everywhere, he said; any trouble and the police were here in minutes. It was hard to find somewhere to live because the black market in apartments had doubled the rents. And learning Swedish here was impossible, because everyone spoke Arabic.

The Husby revolt of 2013, which had been my fiery baptism into Scandinavian life, shone a spotlight on a challenge to the Swedish model that was about to become a prominent question in local and European politics. My conversations with dark-skinned strangers on those long May evenings were an introduction to the country, and also the beginning of an extended period in which I followed the asylum issue for various newspapers at the start of my new life as an immigrant myself – albeit a white, middle-class English one. In interviews for this book with the country's movers and shakers during 2017–18, immigration was a recurring theme; there was a sense that something must be done, urgently, although nobody was really sure what.

"There is a tremendous amount of pushback over the refugees right now – the government and the media are the only people in Sweden who think it's hunky dory," Stu Graham, the former chief executive of construction group Skanska, remarked. Johan Forsell at the Wallenberg's Investor Group lamented Sweden's "insider/outsider problem" – people inside the system were happy, but outsiders couldn't find a way in. Sweden is "not good right now" at integrating immigrants, he said, "we need to improve". Seen in historical perspective, 200 years of peace meant Swedes took a lot for granted, creating a short-sighted approach that if something bad happens, "someone will come to help us," said Carl Bennet, the biotech billionaire. "So we discuss problems in a naive way... The thinking was good on refugees in 2015, but you must plan these things, you must do it in such a way that you can develop it. We shipped water up to our necks. We couldn't handle it."

Recent immigration policy "was a mistake", according to Göran Persson, centre-left prime minister from 1996–2006. "The big group of immigrants that have arrived in the past 10 years – there we have a problem. We are not going to destroy the Swedish model for their sake." Others said finding jobs and homes for tens of thousands of new arrivals meant the model must change. Investment banker Karen Forseke said:

"It was such a huge number of people in relation to our population in such a short period that came into the country. It is causing real challenges and real issues. We are going to have to figure out a way to quickly get them into jobs. We will have to go away from the model if we are to manage this. If we don't manage this well, then we will have serious problems ahead of us. We

are seeing it now in the violence and in the whole areas where people are not working, not being integrated. This means having to accept alternatives to our traditional model of high quality, high pay jobs. Our system is being tested. We have to wake up to it."

In the 1980s and 90s the country managed relatively large flows of refugees from Yugoslavia and Iraq. Can it do so again?

JOBS: IN SEARCH OF A COMPROMISE

Ahmad Saadeha challenges all the stereotypes of a refugee. Just two years after fleeing the war in Syria, the 28-year-old is holding down a job in the IT department at the headquarters of Volvo Group, the global truck manufacturer based in Gothenburg. With his neatly trimmed beard, fashionable spectacles and good shoes, it is hard to believe that he twice crossed the Mediterranean in a rubber dinghy (the first time it sank) and made it to Sweden on forged documents. "I decided I had to take some risks in my life, to think about my children and grandchildren – I didn't want them to have the same things I experienced in life," he says. After he arrived in Sweden in 2015, he waited 15 months for a decision on his asylum application, sharing a room with other refugees in a small village.

133

Out of the blue he got an email from Stockholm's Royal Engineering Academy, who had seen his LinkedIn profile. The Academy had a programme to help skilled refugees, and they encouraged Saadeha to apply – he had a degree in business administration from Damascus University, he spoke good English, and he had experience working for some big companies in Qatar. After numerous applications, he was accepted by Volvo on a 4-month internship. Saadeha describes the feeling:

"It was a moment of surrendering to wonder. You cannot imagine what it is like to be a person with nothing, and to get an opportunity."

It meant getting up at 4.30 am every morning to be at work by 8am. His internship was extended and turned into temporary, and subsequently permanent, employment. It was perfect, Saadeha says:

"I am an active person, a producing, valid person. It has been hectic but it feels so good to have this opportunity. Swedish society has allowed me to do this. I have a commitment to pay back this favour to the community."

"IT WAS A MOMENT OF SURRENDERING TO WONDER. YOU CANNOT IMAGINE WHAT IT IS LIKE TO BE A PERSON WITH NOTHING, AND TO GET AN OPPORTUNITY."

Ahmad Saadeha, *IT department, Volvo Group*

Saadeha was recruited as part of a national programme involving 150 employers and providing around 1,000 internships a year, financed by the government and the Wallenberg family. The aim was to fast-track refugees and other skilled immigrants into work, but there were also benefits for the companies themselves. With the economy growing, and 1.6 million Swedes due to retire by 2025, Sweden would soon be short of tens of thousands of skilled workers, according to Kristian Andersson, Talent Director for Volvo. Moreover, the company was expanding rapidly and needed to employ at least 1,000 workers over the next two years in Sweden alone. "The competitiveness is intense, there is a war for talent. Therefore we see people coming in as extremely helpful to us, they are resources that we need to stay competitive and to stay successful," he said. "We need to embrace the people coming in." The internship programme was an opportunity to test people out. But Andersson had other justifications for Volvo's attempts actively to recruit refugees:

"Companies with a diverse workforce perform better, they have more innovative thoughts and products, so they serve customers better. And foreigners open doors for us in markets where we are not so strong, help us understand those markets better. Without diversity you can only develop to a certain extent. If you grow up in the same house, that's your world – with diversity you see the world. We have a global presence and we need to reflect it. Only 2 per cent of our sales are in this country, we are active

in 192 markets. By bringing in newcomers to Sweden it enriches you, you see a broader perspective, it turns a local company into a global company."

The easiest approach was still to recruit Swedes, Andersson acknowledged – you know the context, the business doesn't need to adjust as much to include them. But he cited studies suggesting that when you have to work a little to explain things, employees get smarter, they are inspired to try new approaches. And it gives them a more objective platform for making decisions: "When you are in a Swedish context it will be a Swedish decision," he said. "The task I have is to sell the internship programme, to give people good arguments why this is a good idea. But we have so many engaged people who are willing to try, willing to take a stand for what we think is good as a company, and who also see the benefits." Although the company had recruited only a few dozen white-collar workers this way, in 2018 it was due to expand the programme to blue collar jobs, mixing internships with training and language lessons.

Here was the Swedish model working well – fast-growing companies focused on world markets, seeing the potential for their businesses of helping refugees into work on the same high wages as everyone else. But would this be enough? In 2016, a large chunk of Swedish business said "No". Only half the recent refugee intake had even secondary education – so what about the other half? Just 5 per cent of jobs in the Swedish economy demanded "no need for special skills", the lowest proportion of all EU countries. Sweden's model of high-skilled, high-wage jobs just couldn't absorb the unskilled refugees, the argument went. Minimum wages in Sweden were twice as high as in most developed countries, making it economically unfeasible to create low-skilled jobs suitable for new arrivals.

You didn't have to be Einstein to see the scale of the mismatch between the productivity levels currently demanded by Sweden's economy, and what most refugees had to offer, said Johan Javeus, chief strategist at Swedish bank SEB. "In the past we have spent a lot of resources on educating the workforce to have high-skilled jobs – this is very difficult to do with the high number of refugees," he said. "It is a shock to the system, and it is hard to see how the old model will not crumble." Sweden was nearing a situation where more than half the total unemployed would consist of people born outside the country. Employment rates among low-skilled immigrants were far lower than those of native Swedes, and the lowest among developed countries – it took seven years or more on average for a new arrival to get work. Joblessness among immigrants was also creating a black economy with low-paid jobs. The Confederation of Swedish Business claimed that 200,000 new jobs could be generated if salaries were frozen or allowed to fall.

In response, Sweden's centre-left rallied behind a defence of the Swedish model. "Sweden is at a crossroads. Therefore the Swedish model needs to be strengthened more than ever," the prime minister declared. Introducing "poverty wages" would deliver a "major blow" to Swedish competitiveness, the Labour minister added. "It is an un-Swedish model with inspiration from southern Europe," where the economies of Spain, Italy and Portugal were based on a far higher proportion of low-skilled jobs, she argued. The trade unions were even more vociferous, accusing the business lobby of "resorting to apartheid" to lower salaries, using "a battering ram to attack workers' rights" and placing a "grenade under the Swedish model". Instead of giving them low-paid jobs, Sweden would have to educate these people, offer them vocational training and move them up the skills ladder.

Proposals to lower minimum wages were nothing particularly new, however – lower starting salaries had previously been proposed as a solution to unemployment among women and young people, according to Patrik Vulkan, a labour market researcher at Gothenburg University. Comparisons between Sweden and the United States, where minimum wages are lower and em-

137

ployment rates far higher among recent immigrants, are misleading, he said, because Sweden had far more refugees, whereas US immigrants were primarily seeking work. Economic migrants are much more likely to have thought about choosing a destination where their skills are needed, rather than just hoping for the best.

Nine out of 10 refugees in the latest wave were aged under 40, so most had a reasonably full working life ahead of them and would repay the investment they required in education and skills, the unions maintained. "The bumble bee shouldn't fly, but it flies really well," Karl-Petter Thorwaldsson, head of LO, the Swedish Trade Union Confederation, told me in the Spring of 2017. "So we have agreed with the employers to negotiate a new agreement on how to get more refugees into work – the typical Swedish way of solving problems is the pragmatic way." It took months to a hammer out a deal, which employers and unions then took to the government. They proposed that businesses should pay as little as 8,400kr (€800, $1,000) a month to hire refugees for up to two years, with the state topping up their pay to the national minimum level in each sector. Private sector agencies would match vacancies to refugees, who would, like apprentices, be allowed paid time off to study Swedish and improve their skills.

Could this idea of subsidised apprenticeships succeed, creating entry-level jobs while maintaining high level wages for everyone else? Patrick Joyce is well qualified to judge – he was a senior adviser on labour markets and integration for Sweden's centre-right government from 2006–2014, and a co-author of New Start, a successful subsidised jobs programme designed to help the long-term unemployed. The preconditions for absorbing the new influx of refugees were encouraging, Joyce said: "So far it looks good – we have economic growth, high employment and labour shortages. But these agreements have failed before." The centre-right had tried a similar apprenticeship scheme to help young people and immigrants, aiming for 30,000 subsidised places; they managed only 700. "The unions and the employers didn't really want it. There was an agreement with the government, but when push came to shove they didn't create these jobs," Joyce said. Also, subsidising work can have unintended consequences. A large share of the taxi drivers in Sweden are immigrants, for example. This is because the taxi companies discovered they could hire most of their drivers through New Start, getting a hefty subsidy from the state. As a result, native Swedes find it harder to become a taxi driver, which is just not fair.

Over the longer term, Sweden is no better or worse than Germany, the Netherlands or other Nordic countries at getting refugees into work, Joyce says. But it is slow at the beginning, with a much higher proportion out of work during their first years in the country. So would the refugee influx force a shake-up in Sweden's unusual labour market? "It's unlikely," Joyce says. Compromise is messy, but it is the Swedish way.

HOMES: NO RETURN TO THE 1960s

The housing market does not work. Our employees cannot find anywhere to live. Fix it, or we will quit Sweden.

This was the blunt message to the government from the founders of Spotify, Daniel Ek and Martin Lorentzon, in the spring of 2016. They were trying to recruit young talent to Sweden from all over the world, but the acute shortage of rental accommodation meant moving to Stockholm was unattractive. "Compare it with cities like New York, London and Singapore where the opportunity to rent housing is very simple," Ek and Lorentzon wrote. "We are therefore forced to note now that if no changes occur, we need to consider expanding more into other countries instead of Sweden."

A few months later, Sweden's Housing Board issued a bombshell estimate of how many new homes the country would need if demand was to be met. Sweden would need to build more than 700,000 new homes by 2025, implying a rate of construction not seen since the 1970s – "totally different" to the pace of house building over the past two decades, the Housing Board said. Adding to the urgency, it said, was unexpectedly high immigration.

The housing crisis in Sweden had been growing for years, but the surge of new arrivals moved it up the agenda. For young Swedes the idea of securely renting or owning their own home had become a disappearing fantasy. According to the Tenants Union, in 2017 almost a quarter of young people in their 20s were still living with their parents, while a similar number were subletting or renting a room. More than half of Stockholm's population – nearly 600,000 people – were registered in the queue for a coveted rental apartment, because the tightly regulated rental market means that rents were relatively low. Getting to the front of the line in central Stockholm took 20 years, while even in suburbs like Husby the waiting time in 2016 was more than a decade. Some who lived in overcrowded accommodation were able to jump the queue, but there was no system of prioritising key workers or people in desperate need of a roof over their heads. Rents in newbuild apartments were significantly higher because construction companies had been exempted from rent controls; low rents often meant properties required renovation and repair.

The result was a thriving rental property black market, with large bribes changing hands to obtain a rental contract. Many tenants exploited the situation by subletting space – when someone advertised a tiny closet in their apartment, there were many applicants. "It is almost impossible for immigrants and new arrivals to penetrate this market – it is all about who you know and how much money you have," said Billy McCormac, head of the Fastighetsägarna property association. Refugees alone would need nearly 40,000 new homes per year in 2015 and 2016, the Housing Board said. Meanwhile, the high demand for homes coincided with cheap loans to produce a house price bubble – property prices rose six-fold in 20 years, with homeowners taking on colossal levels of debt. The ratio of household debt to disposable income soared to become one of the highest in the world. The market expanded when large numbers of tenants were given the right to buy – which in turn increased the shortage of rental properties.

A few months after the Spotify letter, the centre-left government announced a "historic" investment in more housing. The state would make it easier for construction companies to get building permits and planning permission, it would make more land available, and offer billions in subsidies for companies to build low-rent properties in areas where it might not otherwise be profitable to do so. Since 2012, house building in Sweden had been rising steadily, and it continued to do so after the government announced its package of measures. So it is hard to know whether the relatively high number of new homes built in 2017 was connected to government policy. Also, there were warning signs that the higher pace of house-building might not be sustainable – the forecast for 2018 was for a dip in construction, owing to capacity constraints in the construction sector. The government's targets were testing builders to the limit. "Let me put it this way: it's twice the speed of what we are doing today," said Henrik Landelius, head of building at NCC, one of Sweden's biggest construction companies. With politicians promising a quarter of a million new homes in just five years, comparisons were made with the 1960s – the last time Sweden built a lot of homes in a short time. There was talk of a new "Million Programme", echoing the period from 1965 when, to international acclaim, a million new homes were built in just 10 years.

Hopes for a new "Million Programme" are misplaced, says Erik Stenberg, associate professor of architecture at the Royal Institute of Technology. That housing programme, which turned Sweden from having the worst housing stock in Europe to among the best, was the result of careful planning and collaboration over decades, Stenberg says – in contrast to today. The first commission to examine the problem was appointed in 1933, and data collection and analysis continued after the war. Stenberg continues:

"There was a coupling between politics and industry based in the Saltsjö-baden agreement [see Chapter 1], which in turn led to a coupling of quality and quantity – so that we built better as we built more. To do that we had to reorganise the whole of society to produce better housing, which in turn would help change society. Children would have their own rooms, and so get better education, better jobs, then pay more taxes and thereby contribute to the welfare state. Studies were done of how much storage space a typical family would need, and how companies could produce goods to fit into those spaces. IKEA is the prime example of a company that built itself on this standardisation. Lots of flexibility was built into the housing to allow for social change. Production was driven by the idea of 'good living' – if we produce good housing we will get better citizens."

But this building explosion came to an end by the global economic crisis brought on by the 1973 oil price shock, and a sudden shift in Swedish society away from the modernist visions of the 1960s. Although high-rise apartment blocks made up only one-third of the output of the Million Programme, they came to symbolise everything that was considered wrong with it: uniform, standardised, even "inhuman", Stenberg says. This post-modernist backlash, together with the economic crisis, led to a dramatic collapse in house building. Construction companies went bankrupt, key people left the industry or retired, and expertise built up over decades was lost. Even archives were destroyed – the reputation of the Million Programme was so bad that nobody wanted anything to do with it.

As a result, Stenberg argues, 45 years later there is little structural understanding of how to produce a lot of high quality, affordable homes in a hurry without storing up problems for the future. The early Swedish model gave rise to an approach to housebuilding that has long been abandoned. Leaving construction to the market, albeit with blandishments from the state, is an experiment that may work, or that may end in a new crisis, Stenberg says. Indeed, there is also the danger of repeating the other outcome of the Million Programme – producing a lot of new housing that society then turns against. It is precisely the Million Programme apartment blocks of the 1960s and 70s that are now home to Sweden's recent immigrants. So there is justified scepticism that volume alone can overcome the sharp segregation between white and black areas, and the tendency for the latter to become pools of deprivation and discontent.

While more homes and cheaper rents are essential, another set of problems needs to be addressed, says Boel Godner, the Social Democratic mayor of

"IT IS A DANGEROUS DEVELOPMENT IN MANY WAYS. IF YOU FIND YOURSELF OUTSIDE, NOT BELONGING TO SOCIETY, IT IS EASIER TO END UP UNEMPLOYED, OR USED BY ORGANISED CRIMINALS. THAT HAS TO BE CHANGED."

Boel Godner, *Social Democratic mayor of Södertalje*

Södertalje, a city close to Stockholm where more than half the residents were either born abroad or have both parents born abroad. In parts of the district this rises to 85 per cent; in one school just two of its 750 pupils are classified as ethnic Swedish. Famously, since the 2003 invasion of Iraq, the city has accepted more Iraqi refugees than the US and Canada put together. Södertalje became infamous for gang violence in the first decade of this century, but Godner has overseen a successful combination of tough policing and targeted social interventions, and the city now makes headlines again, but for the right reasons.

"The huge migration in 2015 was a wakeup call for the Swedish model – it was like they woke up and found out that it was happening, that so many people were coming from other countries," Godner says. "Suddenly the issues that we were talking about for so long are being taken seriously." For years Godner has insisted that the law enabling refugees to settle anywhere they please should be scrapped, obliging the whole of Sweden to become more ethnically mixed. Planning for each region to take a quota of immigrants – and create sufficient housing to accommodate them – would also increase the chances that refugees would learn Swedish and learn to be Swedes, rather than disappearing into high-density immigrant areas where they are more likely to become cut off from the surrounding society, Godner says.

"If refugees had come to every city it would have been different. At present, so many people end up in segregated areas and have problems learning Swedish, yet that is the key to getting a job. This is why it has to be changed. Every child should go to a school where other children speak Swedish. It has to be solved – it is a dangerous development in many ways. If you find yourself outside, not belonging to society, it is easier to end up unemployed, or used by organised criminals. That has to be changed."

Building more homes is therefore only part of the solution, she says. It makes no sense for areas such as Södertälje to keep on welcoming large numbers of immigrants while there are so many parts of Stockholm that remain whites-only areas. The black market in housing has to be smashed, Godner says, with stiff penalties for people who make money by cramming immigrants into small apartments. "People from other countries should live in every city, that is what makes countries strong and not polarised. Your chance of making it will be so much better to make it if you spend time in a small town with few immigrants while you learn Swedish. Then you can move in an organised way to get a job, an apartment and so on. It may sound hard, but it is the only solution for immigrants to get a good future."

'ICE IN THEIR STOMACHS'

They are known as *eldsjälar* – souls on fire. They organise coffee mornings, jumble sales, children's events, football matches, day trips, legal advice, music evenings, picnics, dances, language classes – anything that brings local Swedes together with the asylum seekers in their midst. Groups like this were initially praised by politicians as the way forward for the whole country. Now they are largely ignored, even sneered at. But under the surface they carry on their painstaking work of integrating the new arrivals marooned in communities all over this enormous country. The government provides asylum seekers with a roof over their heads, a bed and three meals a day. And there, more or less, its responsibility ends. Volunteers have stepped in to try to fill the gaps. Sweden also has an official system of guardians who help young asylum seekers settle in. At the last count there were over 150,000 of these *gode män* – literally, "good people".

Civil society has also mobilised to express concerns about asylum seekers. In January 2016, a young female social worker was stabbed to death by a Somali youth in a home for juvenile asylum-seekers in Mölndal, a satellite of my home town, Gothenburg. The boy was placed in psychiatric care. But the killing led to an outpouring of fears about crime and sexual harassment. Across the city public meetings were packed with hundreds of sceptical, anxious and angry people worried that asylum centres would be sited in their neighbourhoods. With the city experiencing an acute housing shortage, there was also exasperation that refugees were getting any accommodation at all.

This is a live debate within Swedish society. Before 2015, immigration was not widely discussed in public, reflecting an establishment consensus that also treated the anti-immigration Sweden Democrats as political pariahs. To an outsider such a myself, it seemed the debate then boomeranged in the opposite direction, with an extreme sensitivity in the media to any issues connected to immigration and asylum. While this was surely better than sweeping problems under the carpet, there was still a tendency to see things in black and white – opponents of immigration seized on every problem as proof of impending disaster, while supporters dismissed these reports as a racist conspiracy. The situation was not helped by an absence of official statistics on ethnicity and crime, helping to stoke visceral fears that recent immigration is leading to a rise in rape and violence.

There are forces abroad that want Sweden to fail. After the stabbing tragedy in Mölndal, Britain's popular Daily Mail newspaper sent a journalist to the town. His report was titled "The city destroyed by migration: Inside the Swedish town where armed gangs patrol the streets, crime has exploded and a beautiful social worker's murder has shocked Europe." The article claimed that Mölndal was facing a "rising migrant crime wave", its streets "at the mercy of gangs of young men". It even talked about "mass shootings with lots of people killed". It was illustrated with photographs all taken at night, depicting scenes of apparent social desolation.

145

This was my home town, and it was a picture I did not recognise. My in-laws have lived here for 40 years, my wife grew up here. So I spoke to many of the people named in the Mail's article. I found people struggling to cope with a difficult situation and stretched resources, but not the picture of social catastrophe depicted by the Daily Mail. The dark scenes photographed by the newspaper in fact told a story of regeneration – the centre of Mölndal was being totally rebuilt, with bright new office blocks and a gleaming shopping mall. Attractive new homes now look down on the town centre from the hills above. When I met young refugees in the town, I found quiet, sensitive teenagers exploring the potential of their new world. One Somali was training to become a carer for Sweden's elderly, working at MacDonald's to pay for his education. He missed his mother painfully. Another had decorated his bedroom walls with pink butterflies.

As for the "mass shootings", there was a spate of deadly, gang-related violence in a distant part of Gothenburg in 2014–15, but within a year the police had jailed the ringleaders and largely put a lid on it. Sweden has an urgent problem with violent gang crime, but this is symptom of issues that have been festering for years in poverty-stricken ghettos where hope is in shorter supply than the drugs that fund the gangs.

Any rape is an unspeakable tragedy for the victim. Any crime is one too many. But it would have been a miracle if the large influx of destitute, traumatised people from world's war zones had not caused tensions and outbursts. It still takes more than 500 days to get a decision on an asylum application, during which people are crammed into empty buildings wherever they can be found, not allowed to earn money, and unable to speak the language. The fact that there has not been more trouble is testimony to the goodwill of most new arrivals and the people around them. Things are not easy. Across the country, individuals are making choices about how they want Sweden to be, and what they want it to become.

Can the country afford it? Those who welcome refugees often argue that they will benefit Sweden by getting jobs and paying taxes. Opponents say the welfare system will go broke. Both sides are wrong, according to Joakim Ruist, an economist at Gothenburg University and one of the few researchers who has looked at this issue seriously. He estimates on average that each refugee that Sweden takes will cost society €200,000 over the refugee's lifetime. This is not a particularly large sum, but nor is it a positive financial benefit. The uncertainties in the calculation are significant, but Ruist believes that his work has at least prevented politicians from making simplistic claims one way or the other. From 2015 to 2017, the government cut its borrowing and debt fell by about 3 per cent of national economic output, Ruist points out – so the refugee wave did not prevent the government from improving its finances.

At the same time, trust in Sweden's institutions appears to be rising. Each year the respected SOM Institute at Gothenburg University asks Swedes how much trust they have in the way institutions conduct their work. The April 2018 survey showed rising trust in the police, the courts, schools, healthcare, and even politicians. Commenting on the results, Andreas Johansson Heinö, deputy head of the liberal think-tank Timbro, wrote:

"Migration policy can be evaluated in different ways, but it has not caused a systemic collapse, at least not in the eyes of the voters. Voters prioritise schools and health, but at the same time they have relatively high confi-

dence in how welfare works. … In comparison with the political parties, the average voter seems to have plenty of ice in his stomach and been striking-ly stable in his attitudes."

Many of those who argue for tight limits on immigration say that the modern welfare state is likely to be undermined by ethnic diversity because people will start to question the redistribution of wealth to other groups. The jury is out on whether Sweden provides any proof of this hypothesis. Meanwhile, the country's welfare sector needs to hire more than 500,000 new staff over the next 10 years, according to the annual recruitment estimates by the munici-palities and county councils, owing to a rising population of children and the elderly combined with the impending retirement of existing personnel. Those workers need to come from somewhere.

In 1938, the renowned Swedish economist and social scientist Gunnar Myrdal was invited by the Carnegie Corporation to conduct an independent study into "the Negro problem" in the United States. After travelling the country for five years, Myrdal's report, An American Dilemma, detailed the situation of black Americans. His conclusions have echoes in Sweden's debate over immi-gration and segregation today:

"It is in this situation of fear, bewilderment, and insecurity that internal dis-unity can arise. Instead of blaming the real causes, the white majority may put the blame for their difficulties on groups from whom they have tra-ditionally been separated. This is all the easier if there are leaders who, for they own selfish reasons, encourage such splits. Such leaders can rise easily in a democracy and only an alert and interested citizenry can choose between these and honest leaders. Much of European history shows us the internal quarrelling, lack of progress, and general weakness that can result from having a sizeable minority not integrated into the nation or not treated as equals."

SUMMARY CHAPTER 5

So, to sum up: can the Swedish bumblebee make room for more in its nest?

- From the five years from 2012 to 2016 inclusive, Sweden received 370,000 asylum seekers, or 3.5 per cent of its total population, far more per capita than anywhere else in Europe; In 2017 it dropped back to 26,000 – or about the yearly average for the period 2002 to 2011

- For decades, Sweden has struggled to integrate its large refugee population, many of whom live in highly segregated suburbs of large towns and cities

- Sweden's economy has a very low number of low-skilled jobs, making it hard for new arrivals to get a foot on the employment ladder

- There has been a fierce debate over whether Sweden's high-skill, high-wage economy would have to change in order to create entry-level jobs for refugees, which has ended with a compromise between employers, unions and the government

- There is a severe shortage of housing in the country, which has helped to force immigrants into poverty-stricken ghettos where crime can flourish

- The government is trying to encourage a house-building programme on a scale not seen since the "Million Programme" of the 1960s – but in very different circumstances

- More houses alone is unlikely to solve the problem of ethnic segregation

- Sweden is gripped by an intense political debate about how to integrate refugees more successfully into its economy and society; there are forces abroad that want to see it fail

148

CHAPTER 6

VIEW FROM THE TOP: HOW CAPITALISM GETS ALONG WITH THE LEFT

A member of the Wallenberg business dynasty; a former left-wing prime minister; and a former "rock star" Conservative finance minister deliver original insights into how Sweden works

Jacob Wallenberg did not want to be interviewed. Sweden's best-known capitalist oozed boredom, even disdain. One by one he dismissed my list of pre-prepared interview questions, concluding: "To me these are very shallow. And these are the questions you ask? They seem a bit..." – he paused for emphasis – "...off."

We were on the 5th floor of Arsenalsgatan 8c, the address near Stockholm's central waterfront from which the Wallenberg family has directed its business empire for 40 years. It was a grey June morning. A mist of fine rain outside the window added to the gloom inside the office. Interviews with a Wallenberg are like hen's teeth. The family motto, "to be, not be seen", is entirely apt, it does its best to stay out of the public eye.

Nor did Wallenberg want to be photographed. His adviser explained that Jacob doesn't like to be associated with power, so would rather his photo was not taken at Arsenalsgatan – the place reeks of old money. But Wallenberg had chosen this venue himself. If old money was going to talk, it would do so on its home territory. And wearing a good suit. So instead of suggesting we reconvene at the nearest MacDonald's, I decided just to suck it up and let the oracle speak.

This chapter consists of interviews with three men who have each, for significant periods of time, had a hand on the tiller when it came to steering Sweden into the 21st century. There is the voice of big business – Jacob Wallenberg's – then one from the left of Swedish politics, and one from the right. The latter was finance minister for eight years from 2006 to 2014, earning a reputation as "the rock star of Sweden's economy", and only partly because of his trademark ponytail hairstyle. The other was a prime minister from 1996 to 2006 whose domineering leadership helped push through unpopular reforms that played a large role in restoring the country's finances.

As befits people at this level of society, all three men talk with fluency and authority about politics and economics. They have a helicopter view of Sweden, seeing the big picture rather than one or two pieces of the jigsaw. And they weigh every word, anticipating questions and objections – they each have a sense of what is possible in the real world and what is not. While in power they have tested their ideas against reality, helping to take the ideological edge off their views of the world. Each occupied positions where they could be part of taking decisions that actually made a difference. This is what makes them interesting, and important, in terms of understanding how Sweden ticks.

"YOUR VIEW OF SWEDEN IS 40 YEARS OUT OF DATE"

So – back to the grumpy Wallenberg. How did this family build a huge and highly profitable business operation while working under governments that appeared far to the left of anything else in western Europe? How could the left allow one single family to control companies worth 40 per cent of the total value of Stockholm's stock exchange? Part of the answer seems to be an accident of biology. The eldest son of the founder of the business was a highly successful entrepreneur, but he and his wife had no children. In 1917 they decided to donate their money to a non-profit foundation. This became the basis of the Wallenberg approach: family members do not personally control the companies they are involved in, instead they are owned by foundations. These are extremely generous in their funding of research and education – the main foundation, named after the childless Knut and Alice Wallenberg, is the second-largest supporter of basic scientific research in Europe. It has grown to be worth $10 billion and has dished out a total of more than $2.7 billion during its lifetime. The guiding principle is *landsgagneligt*, which means "benefiting the nation", which we briefly encountered in Chapter 3. "We work our butts off in the financial part, but we do it for another reason, and that is the development of Sweden. It is how we have been brought up," Peter Wallenberg Jr, Jacob's brother, told the Financial Times.

153

A consequence of this arrangement is that the Wallenberg family tops the rankings of the most powerful business families in Sweden, and indeed in Europe, but does not appear in rich lists. "That is not to say that we are not doing well economically," Jacob Wallenberg says, stating the obvious. "But our fortunes have nothing to do with the fortunes of the foundations". The Wallenberg sphere currently comprises the industrial holding companies Investor AB and FAM AB, their respective holdings, and 15 non-profit foundations. With dividends form the holdings, the foundations have supported research in Sweden since 1917. Wallenberg is chairman of Investor AB..

"We would call that our ecosystem," Wallenberg says. "The idea was that it would trickle through society and eventually benefit people". What is important in the foundations is *landsgagneligt*, which was typical of that day and age, very nationalistic and Sweden oriented, for Knut and Alice, when they founded the first and biggest foundation. It means when we look at things it has to be to the good of the company, that is part of the bylaws. Hence it is an important part of our thinking. "This general line of thought is something you find not only among the Wallenbergs, but also with "many other business

> Arsenalsgatan 8C, in the middle of Stockholm, has been a fortress of the Wallenberg family for 40 years. The horse is a casting of the sculptures on Saint Mark's Basilica in Venice.

owners" in Sweden, he says, adding that this is a key explanation of why the country has a disproportionate number of world-leading, high-tech companies in relation to the number of citizens. "We are focused, we put a lot of energy into R&D, and we do this over a long time. It seems to work."

For governments concerned that businesses should be giving back to society, and not just thinking about their own short-term interests, this must be a powerful argument. "It is not unimportant when you ask a member of the family how they engage with politicians," Wallenberg confirms. After all, the better the companies do, the more dividends will go to the foundations, and the more goes to Swedish research and development. "That defines when we talk to politicians, when we engage in developing businesses, when we decide whether we should be in Sweden or elsewhere, we are partly coloured by that basic set-up, which we did not decide – it was decided for us 100 years ago, so we have to work accordingly. When I or my cousin or brother wake up in the morning, we think: the better the individual companies perform, the more dividends will go into the coffers of the foundations. That is how we think."

The family businesses have also had to learn to live with, and even benefit from, strong and mostly pragmatic trade unions. Wallenberg is unapologetic in his support for this aspect of the Swedish model:

"It is clear in my mind that a constructive relationship and dialogue with labour is conducive to the positive development of a company; you see ample evidence of this in this country. It boils down to the fact that employee representatives at the end of the day believe in market principles and the market economy. They believe that the sound development of a company is the best provider of maximum number of employment opportunities and the good of their members. Then they also pay respect to the strategic discussions at board level, the decisions that are taken of a strategic nature, and they support them because they see that there are no alternatives. Then they support those decisions when they are implemented in the company."

Wallenberg says that more than once he has seen trade union representatives go to a factory where they themselves used to work and tell the workers that it has to close down. "There has to be give and take, management has to pay respect to employee views. But if you find that balance, it works. I would argue that in this country in 95 out of 100 cases it works very well, and I think it works better than the reverse, funnily enough." He compares it to the way

154

that unions work in Germany, where the most important officials represent the central union and are therefore mainly concerned with the union's interests, not the company's. "It is a completely different culture, and completely different way of working as an employee representative, and it is not conducive to the development of the company," Wallenberg says. "Whereas here in Sweden, everyone most of the time is trying to get the company to work. It is a huge difference."

There is also a "principle of consensus", which from a British or North American point of view ought to be impossible, he adds. Comparing his banking operations internationally, "It was so interesting to see how decisions were made in a Swedish setting, where there were long discussions, consensus was reached, and then off you go. But you empower people, this is very important. I went to my British friends, they were all standing to attention, all waiting to be given an order. There was a huge difference in the culture of how you run companies. That is an important part of our Swedish bumblebee, we have been good at modern management, empowering young people to take decisions on their own and run parts of businesses on their own – that is not a given in many other countries. I would say that is one of the reasons that Swedish companies are at least holding the pace with other companies."

155

Despite the stress on continuity and the long term in the Wallenberg outlook – the family is already grooming a sixth generation of business leaders from among its ranks – Jacob Wallenberg is emphatic that the Swedish model of today is very different from that of the 1970s. In fact, he is frustrated that the country's image abroad is still so strongly linked to that period. This "old Swedish model" was popular abroad because it was so successful, he admits. In the mid 1960s, Sweden was the world's second richest country in terms of economic output per capita. It was then at its zenith after being transformed from a very poor country before the war. Wallenberg still remembers feeling proud at school to read statistics comparing the number of telephones per capita, the number of doctors, teachers and so on, and seeing that Sweden was at the top. But the model that delivered this development contained within it the seeds of its own downfall, he argues. Sweden allowed itself to be sucked into in a "social experiment" by prime minister Olof Palme and the left, Wallenberg says: "That is the old Swedish model, the one that people think is still around, even though it isn't."

Sweden in the 1970s and 80s consumed more than it could afford, Wallenberg says, but also became a highly regulated society: "Probably the single most regulated economy outside the Iron Curtain". Foreigners could not buy Swedish companies, he says, currency controls were second to Venezuela to-

"THERE HAS TO BE GIVE AND TAKE, MANAGEMENT HAS TO PAY RESPECT TO EMPLOYEE VIEWS. BUT IF YOU FIND THAT BALANCE, IT WORKS. I WOULD ARGUE THAT IN THIS COUNTRY IN 95 OUT OF 100 CASES IT WORKS VERY WELL, AND I THINK IT WORKS BETTER THAN THE REVERSE, FUNNILY ENOUGH"

Jacob Wallenberg, chairman of Investor

day, there was only one Rolls Royce in the country and a handful of Porsches, the banks were tightly controlled by the government, and the chair of the Social Democratic Women's Federation – a high profile figure – demanded a ban on satellite dishes because she feared Swedish citizens would be bamboozled by misinformation from free-market media.

The beginning of the end of this model came on October 4, 1983, when there were significant protests from a broad section of middle-class Sweden against a proposal to significantly increase the power of government over business. "The idea was that politicians should decide the ownership and direction of companies, which would have been basically a communistic system," Wallenberg says. Palme's successor then decided to take Sweden into the European common market, soon to become the European Union. "Now comes the real shift for Sweden, where we go from being a very regulated country to one that starts to look at alternatives. Joining the common market, accepting that other forces would have a significant say, was a very, very significant shift in this country's state of mind," Wallenberg says.

And it was not just a shift of mind. After the economic crisis of the early 1990s, Sweden underwent a blizzard of deregulation:

"We went from being the most regulated to one of the most deregulated societies among the industrialised countries, if not the most deregulated. When Americans come here and talk about the Scandinavian model,

the great majority of them still think about the old, very socialistic model, whereas in reality it is hugely different. Today we have a very different system, which explains ultimately why the bumblebee is flying. This shift is the most fundamental part of the explanation. Without it, I am sure we would still be flying, but at a lower height."

The economic results speak for themselves, Wallenberg says. Taxes are still high, he admits: but the scrapping of inheritance, gift and wealth taxes early this century has been a spur for entrepreneurs and creative people. In any case, he has nothing against paying high taxes: "We still pay the third or fourth highest taxes in the world. As much as I am the archetype of a capitalist, I support the principles behind that. I think they tax too highly, I think it is detrimental to optimal economic development, but it is a principal I stand by. Contrary to my American friends, who ask what I have been smoking, I think it is called being affected by your environment of many years living in this country. I support the system of taking care of people."

For Wallenberg, then, the essence of the new Swedish model is a balance between fostering capitalism and taking responsibility for people who struggle to fit in, creating an environment that attracts investment and in which "a desire to take care of the citizens remains, but in a much more moderated form" than under the old model. Failure to do this in the US is part of the reason why Trump became president, he says. In business terms, "the ultimate objective is the same, but there are different models of achieving the same objectives". The jury is out on which is the better way, he says: "There are different ways to run things, one system does not outshine the others. I would argue there is a Swedish or Scandinavian model which is a balance, where on the one hand you try to create the best possible circumstances for economic development – entrepreneurship, innovation, R&D, where education is fundamental – but also a society with a significant sense of responsibility."

"THE NEOLIBERAL WAVE IS OVER"

Everything looks small around Göran Persson. He is 6 feet tall (183cm), but he is also broad, built more like a boxer more than a politician. Perched on a functional office chair in a bland meeting room at JKL, the PR company he joined after leaving politics, he seems too big for the room, while the coffee cups look positively Lilliputian. As a government minister in the late 1980s, finance minister from 1994–96, and then prime minister for the next 10 years, his time in office straddles the collapse of the old Swedish model so disliked

158

by Jacob Wallenberg, and the rise of the new one, which Persson did much to usher in. Surprisingly, therefore, for a prime minister of the left, he agrees with Wallenberg – in the years before the 1990s watershed, Sweden stacked up some major problems. "We had a period in the 70s and 80s when everyone got everything they wanted. There were two coalitions in parliament – one for higher spending, one for tax cuts. They worked together to destroy the public finances. It was a very destructive period. It ended in a collapse, we had to restart it."

The strong unions so beloved of the left were as much to blame for the crisis as anyone else, Persson admits. In fact, they were even "part of the destruction of the Swedish system". But they are a pillar of the model once again: "Now they are back and are part of our model, and it works. We have given the trade unions a special role to play, and we still do, and it works. If you follow the process of wage formation, it is extremely disciplined in Sweden. We have had this as a successful concept for the past 20 years."

In the mid-1990s Persson went to Wall Street as Sweden's finance minister to borrow money to cover a huge hole in the public finances. The visit was traumatic, he recalls:

"I had to explain to them why we had such generous unemployment insurance, why we had such high costs in our primary school system. To go there and do that, and realise that, if I didn't have an answer they would not lend me the money, and if they didn't lend me money I wouldn't be able to finance the welfare society – it was a terrible experience. So for me it was easy to say to Swedes: we must get rid of these deficits as quickly as possible. Strong public finances are extremely important if you want to maintain the model."

The result was a series of big reforms: pensions, wages, the public sector, welfare, taxes:

"We did everything at the same time – we used the crisis. There is nothing as productive as as a good crisis, we really demonstrated this during those years. We realised that if we don't do this we will not be able to defend the Swedish model. The model is not for free, we need to work to pay for it, and to work we need to export, and to export we need to be competitive. Without competitiveness, there is no Swedish model. Without the Swedish model, there is no competitiveness. That is the interdependence."

"THE MODEL IS NOT FOR FREE, WE NEED TO WORK TO PAY FOR IT, AND TO WORK WE NEED TO EXPORT, AND TO EXPORT WE NEED TO BE COMPETITIVE. WITHOUT COMPETITIVENESS, THERE IS NO SWEDISH MODEL. WITHOUT THE SWEDISH MODEL, THERE IS NO COMPETITIVENESS. THAT IS THE INTERDEPENDENCE."

Göran Persson, *former prime minister*

160

The Swedish model itself, says Persson, helped save the Swedish model. Because of "a relatively fair distribution of income" in the country, combined with the assumption that everyone has the right to a good education, good healthcare and a good pension paid for by taxes, people bought into the idea that big reforms were necessary – there was a sense of all being in the same boat, and everyone standing to lose if nothing was done. All the same, Persson's government felt it had to increase taxes quite dramatically on the better off. "They had to pay, and they paid. We had very high taxes, 52 per cent for a couple of years. We survived and we started to cut taxes after that. I was paid politically for this in 2002 [with re-election]. You could see in ordinary life that it worked, it was right. To be able to convince people that we had too do it, we needed to be able to say that there was a fair distribution of the burdens – that was important. Then you are back to the fundamentals of the Swedish model, which is also an idea of fair distribution, not just of the burdens but of the results we create together." The result is that Sweden still combines redistribution with a relatively large public sector, paid for by taxes. "It is still there, it will continue to be there," Persson says.

In turn, redistribution has more broadly positive effects on the economy. A good education for all is not just fair, Persson says, but is also essential for Sweden to be competitive. "We need children and we take care of them, it is even better if they are healthy and well educated – that is the basic idea of the Swedish welfare society. It is more economically relevant now than ever

before, because of the demographic situation. We cannot afford to lose any-one. Once we had a surplus of young people – we don't have that any more, even if we are in a better situation than others." Like other industrialised soci-eties, Sweden's population is ageing rapidly, creating greater demands on the welfare state, with fewer taxpayers to foot the bill. Hence, in Persson's view, the importance of maintaining a high birth rate, which in turn strengthens the economic case for family friendly polices: "We need to support young families, to make it possible to combine a good education and a professional career with the responsibility for two or three kids."

Look at the universities, he says, where women students do particularly well. "If when they graduate we tell them, 'Sorry, now you have to choose: either become a mother or a professional,' then we can be sure that many will become professionals and de-prioritise family life. And we know if that happens we will be in an extremely difficult situation, because a society with-out children is a society that will end up in stagnation." Persson sees greater economic advantages in encouraging women to combine families and ca-reers: societies with children have a bigger domestic market and an orien-tation towards the future, not the past. This is part of his explanation of the Trump phenomenon in the United States: older people looking backwards to a return of something that used to be, "making America great again", instead of looking ahead. This attitude also means searching for someone to blame, creating the potential for dangerous political priorities. "Family friendly pol-icies are thus a tremendous asset," Persson says. "They are part of our wel-fare model and they are a success, they have worked, they have delivered. The future will demonstrate that this is the right way to go, we will become even stronger. It is also important to see the real potential of the systematic and successful Swedish equality movement. It's not only about women, it's about us all – it is not driven by gender, it is driven by modernity, by young adults trying to create a better life for their families. They are all more equally engaged in it than we were, not because they have to, but because they want to."

If it isn't obvious already, Persson is bullish about the prospects for this rel-atively egalitarian, welfare-oriented economy that sees its people as assets, puts them to work, taxes them, and re-invests in their comfort and develop-ment, reinforcing the virtuous circle because people see they get something in return. This future-oriented attitude fosters an interest in modernity, an openness to new technologies, new methods and trends:

"It is modern, it is relevant, it is rational. If you had asked me 10 years ago, I would have been much clearer that there is a threat to the model from our Conservative and Liberal parties. But that was based on the global neoliberal wave. I think the neoliberal wave has come to an end, it doesn't offer any answers to today's problems. On the contrary, where you still try to practice neoliberal polices they often result in populistic responses. The established parties I think realise that the neoliberal solution is not something you can implement in a country like Sweden or Germany or Britain. Ten years ago it was a threat – I don't think they would dare to go for it now. We have had so many good years that the political confrontation is not as sharp as before. People take the model for granted, more or less."

Sweden's openness should include its attitude to immigration, Persson says, but not the "naive policy" of opening its doors to everyone. "You cannot have our model and then tell everyone you are welcome to come here, because our model demands that you take part in the workforce. If you do so, then you are more than welcome. The model works perfectly as long as immigrants work – then we can maintain it." The big group of immigrants that have arrived in the past 10 years are a problem, he says. Will it mean dismantling the model by cutting wages to create more jobs? "I don't think there is support for that. We need to find new measures to do it, with the help of creating public jobs," Persson says.

163

Where the system is failing, he hints, is with its treatment of the elderly – the ones who built the Swedish model. "The pension system has one minor problem – the pensions are too low. We have to solve that. But we can afford to have that discussion now." Unless a solution is found, Persson says, the shared assumption that "we are all in this together" will be undermined, weakening the unwritten agreement between government and the governed that if you pay into the system, it will pay out.

"RECLAIM THE MODEL FOR THE RIGHT"

Anders Borg was just 38 when he took over Sweden's finances in 2006. There followed a helter-skelter ride through drastic tax cuts that would make Donald Trump blush, the global financial crash, deeply unpopular welfare reforms, an astonishing re-election to a second term on a wave of personal popularity, and finally defeat in 2014. Borg's trademark ponytail haircut became a familiar feature of meetings of the global elite wresting with the fallout from the 2008 crisis. But the rollercoaster had one more plunge in store: in the summer of

"WITH THE TYPE OF IMMIGRATION WE HAVE HAD, IT IS PRETTY OBVIOUS THAT THE SWEDISH LABOUR MARKET NEEDS TO BECOME MUCH MORE FLEXIBLE."

Anders Borg, *former finance minister*

2017, Borg was at a party on Stockholm's archipelago where, according to   165
the Swedish papers, he was the worse for drink and behaved outrageously.
As a result, he was forced to step down from some top positions, including at
Swedish investment firm Kinnevik and global banking giant Citi.

When we met in Stockholm's Old Town six months later, Borg did not seem
at all like yesterday's man. He had just been hired by a company developing
digital robots, and had lost none of his charm and ebullience, or indeed his
zest for economics. His starting point is already familiar to us: the mess in
which Sweden found itself in the 1990s. Borg recalled how he suffered an
even bigger shock than Persson when he went to Wall Street in 1995 as a
banking analyst – he was thrown out of an office because its occupant had
just lost a lot of money, and his job, for taking an optimistic view of Sweden's prospects. Sweden had to change. For many right-wingers like Borg,
everything associated with the Swedish model felt oppressive, restrictive, they
called it "GDR Sweden" – a reference to communist East Germany – and saw
an over-regulated, stagnant society similar to the eastern bloc.

But on taking power in 2006, Borg did not intend to throw the baby out
with the bathwater. "It is clear that Sweden had deep economic problems in
the 70s and 80s. But after the crisis in the 1990s we had already started to
change the Swedish model quite substantially. Therefore our thinking back
in 2006 was to develop the strengths of the Swedish model." Indeed, Borg's
prime minister and closest collaborator, Fredrik Reinfeldt, talked of "mending,

not ending" welfare, and declared: "The Swedish people want the Swedish model." The Conservatives even rebranded themselves as a "workers party". Had the right tried to reclaim the Swedish model from the left, I asked? Borg replied: "I think we did that, and I am very happy with that decision, I have no intention of leaving it." The system did not require radical change, he said, and was sufficiently flexible to adapt to changing circumstances:

"We were strengthening features that were already present in the system – we reinforced the work ethic and the entrepreneurial spirit. But fundamentally the Swedish model is a very pragmatic, down to earth way of dealing with the tension between social cohesion and growth ... a very modern way of solving the eternal conflict between equality and expansion, cohesion versus dynamism – the Swedish model is potentially one very efficient answer."

Borg rattled off five fundamental features of Sweden's recipe for capitalism: a free-market orientation with highly unregulated markets, especially in retail, services and welfare; one of the best entrepreneurial climates in Europe; a well functioning labour market with a unique wage-setting process delivering both stability and competitiveness; public spending that aids growth – infrastructure, education, and family policies that enable women to work; and strong public finances. To this, he said, you could add cultural features such as the Lutheran work ethic, high levels of trust and transparency, and the low level of corruption, all combining to deliver economic dynamism while keeping society together. Like Jacob Wallenberg, Borg is happy with the trade unions:

"I think strong unions should be part of the system. I would be happy to have around 80 per cent unionisation in Sweden in two or three decades. Strong unions are the partner of the worker. On the white-collar side they put resources into strategies for wage negotiations that are individual-based, providing statistics and arguments so you can go into negotiation with your boss in a good position. It is a kind of lobby for working people, which I would say is the future role for unions anyway: today real wage increases are pretty small anyway, it is much more about work-life balance."

There were some important caveats. For smaller companies, for example, employment protection legislation was still a major obstacle; Borg said he wanted to see more flexibility to hire and fire. But he was careful to state that employers should not have more freedom to sack people without accepting some responsibility for helping them to be re-hired. Here he pointed to the importance of Sweden's "transition system" that we looked at in Chapter 2, where employers pay into a central fund that helps retrain workers who lose their jobs and gets them back into work. This system was preferable to traditional schemes to help the unemployed, Borg said: "It is much more efficient, it is amazingly good." Look at Saab, he said – the Swedish carmaker was devastated by the 2008 financial crash, but most workers were back in jobs a year or two after the company closed down.

In pursuit of greater flexibility, Borg's government tried to reach a deal in the private sector where unions would win more education for people during their working lives, with companies setting aside resources to re-train workers well before there was any threat of unemployment. The idea was to re-skill people in their 40s and 50s, because over the next 10 or 15 years the technology would be transformed. Essentially, this was a scaling up of the existing transition system, with loans and financing for adult learning, heavy subsidies for retraining foundations, and more flexible unemployment insurance. Borg met with unions 250 times, he says, offering "a lot of money and a lot of benefits" as part of a broad negotiation on the labour market. But it fell apart. Clearly there are limits to the flexibility of the Swedish model.

That failure to re-jig the labour market still haunts Borg, who lists it as a missed opportunity. Moreover, the wage levels and under-sized service sector had become a headache in light of the Borg-Reinfeldt government's second main legacy – the call to "open your hearts" to refugees. We over-did it, Borg says. "It is pretty clear we could not take 160,000 in 2015 without severe tensions. It was absolutely necessary to go in the direction that the current government has done," by closing the borders and cutting Sweden's generosity to the absolute minimum. But he defends the original premise:

"It was a natural starting point. Fundamentally Sweden has a sense that we have a responsibility to be a strong social and humanitarian force both in terms of foreign aid and openness, but also in terms of migration policy. We should punch love our weight when it comes to social responsibility: we stayed out of the two World Wars; we did not have the Finnish experience of being attacked by Russia; most Swedes felt we did too little for the Jews, not allowing them to come out of Germany and Poland. The starting point should be you should do as much as you can, your spontaneous reaction should be to invite people in, and then pragmatically adapt to the new realities."

167

Anders Borg, Sweden's finance minister 2006-14, says the centre right strengthened features that were already present in the system: "Fundamentally the Swedish model is a very pragmatic way of dealing with the tension between social cohesion and growth."

If you have migration from countries like Afghanistan, Somalia and Iraq, where education levels are low and tacit knowledge about the modern workplace is minimal, it is extremely difficult to have an adjustment to the current Swedish system, Borg says – to get migrant unemployment down to 10 per cent is close to impossible without lowering entry-level wages. "With the type of immigration we have had, it is pretty obvious that the Swedish labour market needs to become much more flexible."

Borg regrets that his government's second term was not as radical as the first, and left some important business undone. Housing and the rental market had become an urgent problem. They looked at stock options as an incentive for entrepreneurs, but left it too late: "It is a marginal reform in terms of revenues, but super important in terms of dynamism." Meanwhile, the cost of migration would remain high because integration will continue to be slow. The political stalemate in the country, with minority governments and the far-right holding the balance of power in parliament, boded ill for attempts to make significant changes. But the problems facing Sweden today are manageable, Borg believes – compared with other countries it is still in a sweet spot: "Yes we have problems, yes we should deal with them, but it is not comparable to the 80s and 90s." Borg lists the strengths: the dynamism of the entrepreneurial climate and the high number of startups; the education system that produces highly skilled workers; the overall culture with the high degree of trust functions well. Last but not least, politicians get on with business, and vice versa. Borg defines himself as a typically pragmatic politician who is somewhere in the middle – both a left-wing Conservative and a right-wing Social Democrat:

"A unique feature is that we have a very strong relationship between the business sector and politics. Many business people interact with the Social Democrats now they are in office today, and many business people interacted with the Conservatives when we were in power. This is a small country where most people know each other, and where you normally have very open, well-functioning contacts. That is a good feature of the country. It is a lot easier to be pragmatic when you actually know each other, and it is much less confrontational here because people can actually relate to each other."

IN PLACE OF A CONCLUSION

By the end of the interview, Jacob Wallenberg was in a much better mood. An hour and 10 minutes of explaining the world to a slow-witted foreigner had clearly cheered him up. But it was all rather "on message" – there was nothing particularly outspoken or unexpected. Until my final question, that is. Maybe after such a disciplined and polished performance, Wallenberg had relaxed a little. Or perhaps the question really did touch a nerve. Politics is so important in terms of creating an environment for industry to thrive, I asked, so would a Wallenberg go into politics? "We have no legitimacy," he fired back. What, despite all the wealth the family has generated for Sweden? All the jobs, all that philanthropic largesse? Surely the success family's consistency over generations made it about as legitimate as you could get? Wallenberg chose an unusual example to illustrate his point:

"One of the most important questions we face is young unaccompa-nied minors, refugees, people who are almost unemployable. The labour unions refuse to accept lower wages for that particular group, we have the highest low wage in the world. The trade union federation LO refus-es to change that principle because they say it will destroy the whole set up. I argue that you have to find a salary level where people are willing to employ people who are today unemployable, to put them to work and education, rather than society having to pay in financial support. I find it quite revolting, frankly speaking, that we can't find a way around this. I can-not as a Wallenberg stand up on this question because I cannot – given that I am a successful capitalist – be viewed as challenging the salary lev-els of employed Swedes. I would have zero legitimacy doing that, and it would erode my overall legitimacy. So I get stuck in a corner where I can-not move. That is just an example of why it is difficult for a Wallenberg to engage in politics."

171

So Sweden's most powerful capitalist felt "stuck in a corner" after all, forced into silence on an issue that was filling the newspapers and airwaves with heated debate. That is the flip side of strong unions, consensus, give-and-take, and a balance between labour and capital – capital needs to tread care-fully on sensitive issues. Would Jacob Wallenberg himself like a political role, I asked? "I think there should be much more back and forth between business and politics," he said. "We don't have that tradition, unlike Britain or the US, which is a great shame because it means business has a very limited under-standing of politics, and vice versa. It would be great with much more of an exchange." That sounded as close to a "yes" as I was going to get.

SUMMARY CHAPTER 6

So what have these three big-hitters in Sweden's economy revealed about the country where each has exercised considerable power?

• A pre-eminent figure in Sweden's best-known business family identifies some of the defining features of the Swedish model that we have explored earlier, such as the role of the unions, the value of consensus, shared responsibility for the wider society, and the importance of a long-term outlook in business

• That long-term outlook extends to funding a great deal of basic research, which also helps the relationship between business and politicians

172

• The people who run Sweden see the 1980s as a watershed, after which the country modified important aspects of its model, leading to a positive transformation

• Strong welfare policies – education, healthcare, childcare, pensions – are seen by people at the top as good for business, with broadly positive effects on the economy

• A danger in cutting back on welfare is the potential for fomenting populist movements, because of a breakdown in trust between government and the governed

• The essence of the new Swedish model is a balance between fostering capitalism and taking responsibility for people who struggle to fit into it; a fair distribution not just of the burdens when things go wrong, but of the benefits that wealth creation brings; and a pragmatic solution to the tension between social cohesion and economic growth

• Mainstream right-wing opinion in Sweden claims the Swedish model for its own

> Statue to August Palm (1849 – 1922), Social Democratic pioneer, outside LO's headquarters.

CHAPTER 7

'FREEING THE TIGER': VOLVO, CHINA AND THE NEW SWEDISH MODEL

Sweden's love-hate relationship with big cars; how an upstart Chinese company overcame local resistance to acquire a jewel in Sweden's industrial crown; why the takeover worked, when Ford's didn't; Volvo's new SUV as a metaphor for the new Swedish model

Never before had a mung bean seen active service in the class war. When one of these tiny, hard legumes is placed inside the valve of a car tyre, and the cap partially screwed back on, the bean depresses the poppet sufficiently to make the tyre slowly deflate. On a warm night in July 2007, a handful of activists slunk through the streets of Östermalm, a wealthy area of downtown Stockholm, each with a handful of mung beans or gravel and an intention to deflate the tyres of so-called "city jeeps", the Swedish nickname for SUVs – those very big cars that other people drive. By the end of the night, 60 of these symbols of power and status were in a state of feeble detumescence. Owners returned to find a leaflet under the windscreen wipers, which declared:

Your City Jeep Kills
We have let the air out of one or more tyres on your city jeep. Do not take it personally. It's your SUV we do not like. You are probably aware of the amount of gasoline it uses, so we don't need to tell you. But what you either do not know, or fail to understand, is that all the gasoline you burn driving your jeep around the streets has devastating consequences

for others. ... In the end, climate chaos will kill us all – rich and poor. This will not happen if we sharply cut our carbon dioxide emissions. Now. Not tomorrow. Therefore we have disabled your city jeep by letting the tyres down. Because you live in a city with good public transport, you won't have any trouble getting where you need to go without your SUV.

The Indians in turn responded that there was simply no need for these "monster cars" that put pedestrians, cyclists and indeed the whole of humanity at risk. SUVs had only one purpose: status for their owners, they wrote in a popular newspaper. The extra tons of metal on the roads caused fuel consumption up to four times more than a fuel-efficient car, but this didn't concern the owners as they usually had a lot of money. "Take Volvo's popular city jeep, the XC90. It costs around €50,000, weighs over two tonnes and guzzles over a litre of gasoline every 10 km," the Indians claimed.

By taking aim at the XC90, the Indians were targeting the nation's flagship car maker. Volvo was late to the SUV party – the XC90 was its attempt to catch up with a market that was soaring in the USA and beginning to take off at home in Sweden itself. For the global car industry, SUVs were proving to be one of the most effective ways to increase profits. The 1990s had seen ever bigger and more luxurious cars, tapping into growing demand. Volvo's XC90 entered this market in 2002. Sweden already had a reputation for having the largest and most fuel-hungry cars in Europe, partly because Swedish drivers wanted extra-safe vehicles due to the risk of collisions with moose. Also there were no tax incentives for reducing car size and fuel consumption, so the most common Swedish-made models were already relatively large.

When Volvo presented the forerunner of the XC90 at the Detroit motor show in 1997, it seemed like a natural progression from the V70XC ("cross country") version of its midsize saloon. But still the SUV seemed to sit oddly with Volvo's values. "The target has been to find a design that is not as 'macho' as that of many other SUV models in the segment," said Peter Horbury, the company's chief designer. "We prefer to talk about a masculine appearance, a design that creates a sense of security. This is important in view of the fact that many SUV buyers are women who like the feeling of safety and control."

In market terms, the XC90 came not a moment too soon. SUVs made a breakthrough on the Swedish car market in 2002, the same year that the XC90 went on sale. New buyers were mostly urban and suburban dwellers, attracted by the car's associations with outdoor life and prosperity, and by the sense of safety. These had made SUVs an attractive alternative to the sports car trend set by young urban professionals in the 1980s. While the total car

HISTORY HAS MANY EXAMPLES OF INVADERS ADOPTING THE CULTURES OF THE CONQUERED, RATHER THAN IMPOSING THEIR OWN WAYS, WHETHER IT IS THE VIKINGS CONVERTING TO CHRISTIANITY IN THE BRITISH ISLES, OR THE MANCHU ADOPTION OF ASPECTS OF CHINESE CULTURE AFTER THE FALL OF THE MING DYNASTY. IN ASSIMILATING VOLVO, HOWEVER, CHINA'S CORPORATE RAIDERS WERE CLEAR FROM THE START – THEY WOULD LET SWEDES BE SWEDES, AND CHINESE BE CHINESE.

market in Sweden grew by a few per cent in 2002, sales of what were now called city jeeps increased substantially more.

Swedish motoring journalists were initially sceptical. They saw these big cars as dangerous to other road users, and asked why anyone actually needed a car like this when ordinary saloons would do just as well. Presenting the new XC90, one magazine wrote that a Volvo SUV was a contradiction: the company sought an image based on safety, environmental concern, sportiness and slick Scandinavian design, while SUVs were intrinsically "dangerous, thirsty and heavy". A leading member of the Road Safety Council compared Sweden's fleet of vehicles with the rest of Europe and concluded it was already "worst in class" in terms of carbon dioxide emissions. A so-called "penalty tax on city jeeps" was debated in parliament and the media.

The Indians of the Asphalt Jungle seem today like a rather gentle, Swedish response to a very Swedish dilemma – the nation's car maker was caught up in a global trend that played to the country's historical preferences for big cars but clashed with its growing self-image as green and responsible. It was Scandi direct action in which nobody was hurt and nothing was damaged, no windscreens smashed or paintwork scratched, an attempt to start a debate rather than physically block the streets or destroy the enemy. The Indians called off their protests after a few months, citing a dip in SUV sales but also the risk that drivers were setting off without noticing that a tyre was flat, with the potential for accidents.

In fact, much bigger forces were about to hit demand for SUVs in Sweden and around the world. The financial crisis of 2008 smashed into the global car market like a bull moose hitting a Fiat Panda. But even as sales deflated like the tyres of Yank tank on a narrow Östermalm street, far away in Beijing a wealthy entrepreneur was planning an audacious bid for Volvo that would relaunch the XC90 as the saviour of Sweden's car industry.

From the point of view of this book, the story of Volvo, an iconic Swedish brand and a major employer in my home town of Gothenburg, is interesting because it represents an extreme clash of economic cultures in which Sweden came out on top, benefiting both the company and its Chinese owners. History has many examples of invaders adopting the cultures of the conquered rather than imposing their own ways, whether it is the Vikings converting to Christianity in Britain, or the Manchu adopting aspects of Chinese culture after the fall of the Ming dynasty. In assimilating Volvo, however, China's corporate raiders were clear from the start – they would let Swedes be Swedes, and Chinese be Chinese.

.

THE PEASANT AND THE MOVIE STAR

Li Shufu was accustomed to thinking big and winning difficult arguments. Born into a farmer's family, he went straight from school into business in 1984 with a tiny sum from his father. By the age of 21 he owned a factory making refrigerator components, creating his Geely brand. In the mid-1990s, expensive imported motorcycles were popular in China, and Li somehow persuaded the government to let him bail out a struggling, state-owned motorcycle factory in Hangzhou. Before long, Geely motorcycles were being sold in 22 countries, including the US and Europe, and were China's top brand. Just three years later, having overcome opposition from all quarters, Li became China's first private producer of motorcars. At one point, according to the *China Daily*, he begged an official: "Please let me try. It is my dream. I'll pay for everything and take all the risks. Just give me an opportunity to win or lose on my own." At the turn of the millennium sales of Geely compact cars began to take off in China and abroad. In 2006 Geely established a joint venture in Shanghai to manufacture the iconic London black taxi cab.

But Li had even bigger fish to fry. He believed that Volvo could give him the innovation, branding and technology he needed to propel Geely, and China's

< Making cars at Volvo: the company has thrived under Chinese ownership.

auto industry in general, into global markets. Volvo at the time was owned by Ford, the US multinational. Li began courting Ford's leadership, but Geely was both a novice and a minnow: in 2005 its sales were just 140,000 at the budget end of the market, while Ford was selling more than 6 million cars a year. Early in 2008, at the Detroit auto show Li met a senior Ford executive, who was courteous but appeared put off by Geely's size. Just a few months later, the global financial crisis struck, giving Li an opportunity that would, in his words, be like "a world-famous movie star marrying a peasant in China". In February the following year the news broke that Geely wanted to bid for Volvo, and that Ford was keen to offload its loss-making subsidiary to focus on the crisis in its home market.

A summer of speculation was followed by an autumn of Swedish contempt and outrage, as it emerged that Geely was the front runner to take over their national treasure. Most of the Swedish media was caustic, with a great deal of scepticism that an unknown rickshaw of a company could save this sleek Scandinavian limousine with 80 years of history behind it. Geely's acquisition was presented as damaging or even dangerous, with dire predictions of the collapse of the Volvo brand, the closure of its mighty Torslanda plant in Gothenburg, the loss of technology to China, and mass unemployment for Volvo employees and subcontractors on Sweden's west coast. It seemed impossible that Western and Chinese company cultures could successfully combine. "The Chinese car industry is primitive and has nothing to teach Volvo," sneered one newspaper motoring columnist. "Unless it's about how to deal with unions – the communist dictatorship does not allow a free trade union movement." Wrote another: "Geely can kill Volvo's strengths. ... There is only one plus: the ability for Volvo to grow rapidly in China. The uncertainties and risks are far greater."

A major fear was that the Chinese would steal technological secrets – a concern fuelled when Geely exhibited what looked like a replica Rolls Royce Phantom at the Shanghai auto show in April 2009. Volvo's unions said they were worried that subcontractors would cease selling Volvo the latest technology, fearing it would be stolen, and leading to a loss of competitiveness and jobs. The relationship between Volvo and its suppliers was a long-term partnership based on trust, argued Magnus Sundemo, head of the engineers trade union at Volvo. Geely, Sundemo alleged, was a different animal, hiding its ownership structure behind unlisted companies in the Cayman Islands. "It's scary," he said.

Sundemo, a soft-spoken man with a Tiggerish smile, became a tireless agitator against a Geely takeover. Shortly after his retirement from Volvo's Board, he recalled in 2017:

"I was one of the biggest opponents of the Chinese, I was out in the media and TV and all over the place, talking about the risk of this company just making copycats of Western cars. What could they add or bring to the table? I was scared that the suppliers would disappear when they understood they would be doing business with a Chinese company. Audi and others had got fantastic results by not being Chinese. There were good opportunities to grow in China without being owned by the Chinese."

For these reasons, Volvo's owners should be based in the Nordic region, he believed – they should be people who understood "the Volvo spirit" and its vision of cars with high environmental and safety performance. The engineers union called on the government to step in and find a Nordic owner. Sundemo took the initiative to create a rival, management-led Swedish consortium to challenge Geely. Consortium Jakob, named after Volvo's first ever model in 1927, was fronted by Sören Gyll, a former boss of Volvo Group in the years before the company was divided and its automobile division sold to Ford in 1999. Gyll it was who had used his influence on Volvo's board in the early 1990s to prevent a merger with French car maker Renault. The workers had wanted to keep Volvo Swedish, Gyll said. "When we broke with Renault, I remember the atmosphere we managed to create afterwards – I hope we'll be able to do it's something like that again this time."

Consortium Jakob called on the company's workers to become part owners by chipping in two months' wages. Swedish car dealers were also offered shares. Magnus Sundemo recalls:

"We went around all the rich people in Sweden to ask for support. We also had an idea to let all the employees become part owners, a cooperative. But the managers didn't deliver. If we had gone to the Swedish public we could have raised the money – I got a lot of letters of support from all over Sweden at the time. But none of the politicians believed in us. They had been through the docks crisis in the 1970s when the shipbuilders went down, the government had stepped in and it was a disaster. They didn't want to do that again. So we weren't able to raise enough money."

Already, however, attitudes among those closest to Geely had begun to change. The blue-collar workers union IF Metall was led at the time by Stefan Löfven, who five years later would become Sweden's prime minister. In the early autumn of 2009, just as Consortium Jakob was unravelling and the dream of a Swedish buyout was falling apart, Löfven signalled a more positive attitude. His union was in touch with Geely, which had understood the Swedish model, he told newspapers. "We are careful to emphasise that, to succeed, you must have good contacts with the employees so that they get a high level of participation. [In this way] the Swedish model gives a competitive edge. Geely says that they understand this, and that when production takes place in Sweden, it must be done on the terms that apply here. We naturally want to develop that reasoning," he said. What Löfven took from his discussions with the Chinese was that production and development would remain in Sweden. "They see the value of Swedishness, which has to start in Sweden."

Sundemo and his engineers also met with Geely's top management. It was an open meeting, Sundemo said at the time, during which they got some answers. Li told them he was listening to the union. "It felt good," Sundemo said. Now he himself was beginning to feel the heat: his insistence on Swedish ownership had attracted accusations of xenophobia towards the Chinese, and he was forced to explain himself. Increasingly it looked as though Geely would win the bidding war and become Volvo's new owner. Sundemo told me:

"I was in a critical position. People were asking: will I resign? But we visited China and met Li Shufu. I said to him: we both have something in common, we both love the company. Li asked if I would support the takeover – otherwise he wouldn't go ahead. There had been serious problems in South Korea when the Chinese did a takeover, maybe he didn't want to repeat that. Then he told us about his plans for 'freeing the tiger' at Volvo."

Li was known for a somewhat poetic choice of words. Sundemo was not the first to hear him describe Volvo as a "tiger" that he wanted to set free. "Free the tiger? I thought it was bullshit at the time," Sundemo says. "I didn't understand at all what he meant. But he saw the strength in the organisation. He took a tremendous risk when he bought Volvo." When the deal went through early the following year, Li vowed to respect Volvo's independence. He promised the workforce that he would preserve Volvo's big operations in Europe's high-cost, low-growth car market, arguing that growth in China would allow Geely to save jobs in areas such as research and development.

"Geely is Geely and Volvo is Volvo," Li said. "We should not be characterised as father and son, rather as brothers, and we want to benefit from each other's strengths." Later he told the Financial Times: "We gave them back their freedom."

AN ELEPHANT-SHAPED SNAKE

At the time, Geely's purchase of Volvo from Ford in 2010 was one of the most high-profile takeovers by corporate China, and it still serves as a test case for Beijing's industrial ambitions. The deal is part of the debate that rages over China's overseas acquisitions, which are often subject to close European and US scrutiny. At the higher levels inside Volvo itself there was an acute sense of the company's vulnerability. What happened, however, came as a surprise to everyone.

"I believe that when Geely acquired Volvo they did so for the brand, the technology, the engineering, the market presence. The one thing they had – and that was misunderstood by many – was a huge respect for Swedish

"WHEN GEELY ACQUIRED VOLVO THEY DID SO FOR THE BRAND, THE
TECHNOLOGY, THE ENGINEERING, THE MARKET PRESENCE. THE ONE
THING THEY HAD – AND THAT WAS MISUNDERSTOOD BY MANY –
WAS A HUGE RESPECT FOR SWEDISH INNOVATION, ENGINEERING,
PEOPLE, AND THE SWEDISH BUSINESS MODEL."

Tom Johnstone, *Board member at Volvo and other Swedish corporations*

innovation, engineering, people, and the Swedish business model," says Tom   185
Johnstone, one of the European corporate heavyweights brought in by Geely
to help steer the ship. Although a Scot, Johnstone is a veteran of Swedish
industry, the former boss of ball-bearing maker SKF with a string of Swedish
board positions under his belt. All its life, Volvo cars had been a division of a
bigger industrial group – first as part of Volvo AB, which made trucks, earth
movers and marine engines, and then a division of Ford, Johnstone says.
Now it became a company in its own right, giving it a shot of energy.

Ford had brought some financial discipline, but it wanted Volvo to be part
of the bigger structure, says Lex Kerssemakers, the Dutch head of Volvo in the
US who, when we spoke in 2017, had been with the company for 25 years.
Volvo management felt under siege by the Americans, he says: "Engineers
and people here felt limited in their freedom, we had to comply with rules not
based on our values and ethics – instead, there was hierarchy, processes, law
and order, meetings, formalities. Swedes want to be independent, they want
to be left alone, they don't bother other people too much. When you take
away their independence they start to revolt, and that happened a little under
Ford." The Chinese were clever, Kerssemakers says – the new owners didn't
make a revolution, but created momentum:

The end of the assembly line at Volvo's Torslanda plant. The Chinese strategy for "freeing the tiger" – running Volvo Cars as an independent organisation within Geely, with unprecedented freedom and access to capital – delivered results.

"That was a huge difference, it triggered a lot of dynamism. Follow your business guts, they said. Geely gained a lot of respect because they trusted Volvo, they had the patience and vision to allow us to do our job. We know how to make cars, the competence level is extremely high. So the Chinese said: you are the knowledgeable partner. What they brought was an entrepreneurial attitude – follow your intuition, don't try to calculate everything. Many of us felt extremely obliged not to disappoint the major shareholder."

Under Ford, Volvo had adopted a tortoise strategy — withdraw into your shell, pull in your legs and head and allow the Ford strategy to wash over you, says Carl-Peter Forster, a German executive who had worked in the auto industry all over the world before he joined Volvo in 2013, helping to lead companies such as BMW, Opel, Saab, General Motors, Jaguar Land Rover and Tata Motors. He says:

"The American automotive companies believe it is best to tell everyone exactly what process to follow every day. So you push back. I think Volvo has started sticking arms and legs out again and is moving forward confidently again. Geely supported us financially, but didn't rescue us – that changed the mindset inside the organisation. The air is clear, we can move forward. You have to allow the organisation to build a great product, and allow the people to decide what is a great product that suits our brand."

The approach was similar to that of the new Indian owners who took over Jaguar Land Rover at around the same time that Geely bought Volvo, Forster says. A more entrepreneurial culture came in and said: I believe in the brand, lets unleash the organisation. "Initially you have to fund it, but in both cases it worked. It was a huge investment for Geely, and they are a smashing hit," Forster says. The Chinese owners were not benevolent, it was all about business performance, about moving faster and growing, being more entrepreneurial, about drive and speed: "We didn't have that under Ford – how could we? We were told which model we could do."

This was what "freeing the tiger" looked like in practice. "Li Shufu is pushing like hell – we will never be going fast enough for him," says Johnstone. "It is a lesson for the rest of Sweden – we need to go faster. Those companies who are open to Chinese competition already realise that. ... The Chinese can build a city for 10 million people in the time it takes for us to build a bridge."

Magnus Sundemo, the union leader and arch sceptic of the Chinese, now admits that his fears were groundless. "Nothing of that happened," he says.

On the contrary, when Geely first took over and were making changes at the top, they sacked a lot of managers – with Sundemo's assistance. "I didn't tell them who to sack, but I advised them. In a sense, that was the Swedish model," he says. Sundemo remembers the first Board meeting under the new boss, when Li started reciting poetry:

> "It was both exciting and scary. They came in with a philosophy of handing control back to Volvo. That was a brave step. Geely gave the CEO and top management freedom to do what they wanted, and they were supportive, instead of asking lots of questions like Ford did, when every decision was scrutinised. ... Ford put in controllers, a mega matrix organisation. They had all these managers in human resources, research, production and finance, to interfere in the organisation. Ford had a lot of cash to throw around, but no ideas about how to develop the industry."

Freeing the tiger might be more than a catchy slogan, it seemed. The Chinese strategy of running Volvo Cars as an independent organisation within Geely, with unprecedented freedom and access to capital, delivered results. After an initial slump in 2011–12, Volvo rebounded. Its profit margins nudged up towards those of the big three German brands that are seen as Volvo's main competitors — Audi, BMW and Mercedes. Sales hit a record at more than half a million cars in 2015, and continued to climb. Its first new models under Chinese ownership were well reviewed. Development times were slashed – in 2010, it took Volvo 44 months to develop a new car; five years later it was down to 30 months. Instead of extracting a dividend, Geely invested all the cash back into the business, spending $9bn on developing new models, engines, and platforms.

Before the Chinese takeover, Volvo had no manufacturing facilities outside Europe; now it has three plants in China and one in the US, while China has become its biggest market. Its new R&D company CEVT went from zero to more than 2000 highly skilled employees in Gothenburg in the blink of an eye, bringing together an international team of designers. "The suspicious view [of the Chinese] gradually disappeared," Christer Karlsson, professor at Copenhagen Business School, told the Financial Times. Sundemo says: "We could never have made the investments that were made under Geely if we had remained under Ford. At no time did we come close to expanding so fast and taking such brave decisions on new products." In the words of Hans Enocson, former CEO of GE in Sweden: "Ford didn't invest in Volvo, they just milked it." In contrast, Geely was a very different owner.

It is tempting to see Geely and Volvo as a story of happily ever after. This tectonic shift in the Swedish and Chinese business landscape seems to have given birth to a lush atoll in a clear blue lagoon, without any accompanying tremors, eruptions or earthquakes. This is not the case. Cars are a cutthroat business. Throats were cut. Li infamously sacked his first appointed CEO, Stephan Jacoby, in 2012 while the latter was still in hospital after suffering a stroke. Jacoby was popular with staff for his love of cars and unwillingness for Geely to get its hands on too much Swedish technology. Pehr G. Gyllenhammar, a former head of Volvo Group, recently described Volvo's fate as a tragedy. "I think they've ruined the whole of Volvo since I left, dismantled the largest industry in Sweden in a hurry, without getting anything for it. ... There are many who are extremely pleased, but not the Swedish people, who have enormous loyalty."

For Glenn Bergström, head of the blue-collar union at Torslanda, the changes have been part of a gradual decay of the Swedish model. To him, the fate of nearby Saab still hangs over Volvo like a shadow. Hit by the same crisis that drove Ford to sell Volvo to the Chinese, Saab failed to find a buyer with deep enough pockets and went bankrupt in 2011. Thousands of jobs were lost. "We didn't use to fear unemployment, now we do," Bergström says. "If something should happen to Volvo Cars there is not a chance in hell that they could take care of that, we would be in big trouble in this region."

So how does the story look from the Chinese side? At the time of the acquisition, the media were fond of quoting a Chinese expression that Geely buying Volvo was "like a snake swallowing an elephant". The simile referred to the differences in size between the two companies, rather than any anthropomorphic features of the animals in question. But after the event, the phrase seems more appropriate as an image of an elephant-shaped snake, its thin skin stretched over something that is still clearly an elephant.

In his simple, oak-panelled office at Volvo's low-ceilinged headquarters in Torslanda, Peter Zhang, who played a central role in Geely's acquisition and was Shufu's spokesperson, takes a big picture view of the process:

"We are dealing with the real world. Companies are just organisations of people. People have roots, they have been brought up in their own ways, immersed in their own cultures. So it's all about how you have a company style or culture that brings the best out of people. Of course, there have been culture clashes, this was inevitable. But the owner is a sensible guy and he has respect for Volvo's culture and core values. He has established

"WE ARE DEALING WITH THE REAL WORLD. COMPANIES ARE JUST ORGANISATIONS OF PEOPLE, PEOPLE HAVE ROOTS, THEY HAVE BEEN BROUGHT UP IN THEIR OWN WAYS, IMMERSED IN THEIR OWN CULTURES. SO IT'S ALL ABOUT HOW YOU HAVE A COMPANY STYLE OR CULTURE THAT BRINGS THE BEST OUT OF PEOPLE."

Peter Zhang, *key figure in Geely's takeover of Volvo*

192

a very good governance structure, so Volvo has been governed by an independent board. When we took over in the beginning we said Volvo will be governed independently. 'Geely is Geely, Volvo is Volvo' – that was the catchphrase. So the board has been trusted to make decisions with the support of the owner. We have had a lot of strategic projects between Geely and Volvo, with people working together, so I have overheard comments about the other organisations, and people might feel a little frustrated when it comes to understanding each other. But these sorts of tensions over time have become fewer and fewer, people are trying to find ways to understand each other and work with each other."

Zhang got closer to this high-wage, high-welfare nation in 2010, finding it remote and very different to China – "more socialist" than many other countries in terms of the value system and "the consultation culture", he says. Despite the high costs, there was no question of closing production and moving it to China. It is more about value generation, he says:

"You need to consider a lot of things. The costs going forward will level out – through productivity gains, higher levels of automation and so on. It has turned out to be good. We didn't even think of reducing the manufacturing footprint in Sweden in 2010, and there is even less reason to think about that now."

Zhang met the former union boss Stefan Löfven once more after Löfven had become prime minister. "When we saw him again he was very pleased," Zhang recalled. "He said we had delivered what we promised."

"THE REPTILE ALWAYS WINS"

I was handed the keys inside a huge subterranean garage. It was like a museum of Volvo's past and future. Under tailored tarpaulins, or just resting moodily, were historic models side by side with the latest beasts to roll off the production line a short distance away. Here was an onyx black Volvo XC90 T6 Inscription. Mine for a week. "Just bring it back in one piece," said a technician as he waved me away.

I was behind the wheel of the car that exemplifies Geely's ambition for its Swedish investment. This machine bore little relation to the old XC90 whose tyres were deflated by environmentalists 10 years earlier. It was the second generation, redesigned from top to bottom, the quintessential product of combined Chinese energy and Swedish expertise. The XC90 is "the ultimate proof" of the takeover's success, says Lex Kerssemakers, Volvo's US boss. Under the new owners, he says, "there was an eagerness to show that we are incredibly good at making cars. We were the leading ones again, we will show we can make the best cars in the world. The result is the XC90, which is beating the shit out of the competition." Likewise, Magnus Sundemo insists: "The XC90 is Swedish. Our big idea was to build on the history, the good things – safety, environmental quality, Nordic design, and to go the full way, to motivate people."

There was a great deal riding on its success. Not only was the XC90 the company's first all-new model under the new owners, but the launch followed billions of investment in new components and factories. The feeling among senior Volvo executives, expressed frequently in media interviews, was that they were not just launching a new model, "they were in effect launching a new company," the Financial Times reported. Within two years of its first appearance in 2014, one in five of the cars sold by Volvo was an XC90. Falling oil prices and rising driver appetite had led to a surge in SUV sales, accounting for a quarter of cars sold by all automobile makers across Europe. "We have taken a step into the premium league," Volvo announced. Profits were up, and the XC90 was a major contributor.

But my first impression of the XC90 was an anti-climax. I am not a car person, I prefer a bicycle or a boat. Cars have four wheels and an engine and they get me from A to B – who cares if they are big or small, premium or Prius? I have managed most of my life without owning one at all. Here I was driving just another car, but bigger. I felt self-conscious. What would the neighbours think of this ostentatious symbol of personal wealth that had suddenly appeared outside our house? What would it say about the sort of person I am? Someone with money to burn, I supposed. And a small penis. Enormous cars with darkened windows like this are driven by gangsters in Moscow, not wimpy journalists.

And then, slowly, I began to understand. Nought to 60 mph in around six seconds. It felt like I was driving a sports car the size of an armoured personnel carrier. My younger brother-in-law, who is faster and sharper than me at everything sporty, tried to race me from a standing start in his VW Polo. Within moments he was a small speck in my rear-view mirror. Other drivers appeared to be scared. I began to recognise the precise moment they noticed me coming up behind them – a small swerve of panic as their instinctive reaction was to get out of the way. And then they got out of the way.

I began to feel that I owned the road. I went through a red light without noticing. The car that had right of way gave a brief and half-hearted beep on his horn, it was almost apologetic – I had priority. My men friends stroked the XC90 like it was a thoroughbred race horse and begged to drive it. Young women asked to sit in the front and – honestly, this really happened – whooped and squealed with each surge of power whenever my right foot stamped on the accelerator and we flew effortlessly past everything else on the road, cushioned by the extraordinary suspension, and also by the sense that we were almost entirely safe.

The French anthropologist and consumer psychologist Clotaire Rapaille, who worked for Chrysler in the 1990s, developed an analysis of how SUVs appeal to people's most primitive instincts. Drawing on the work of Carl Jung, the Swiss founder of analytic psychology, Rapaille divides people's reactions to a commercial product into three levels of brain activity: there is the cortex, for intellectual assessments; the limbic, for emotional responses; and then the reptilian, which he defines as reactions based on "survival and reproduction". He concluded that SUVs are "the most reptilian vehicles of all because their imposing, even menacing appearance appeals to people's deep-seated desires for survival and reproduction", according to New York Times reporter Keith Bradsher, who wrote a book about the SUV phenomenon. The Jeep Grand Cherokee launched in 1992 was a result of Rapaille's work, as was the new front on the Dodge Ram Pickup in 1994. These cars would make other motorists "want to get out of your way", he said. "My theory is the reptilian always wins", Rapaille wrote. "The reptilian says, 'if there is a crash, I want the other guy to die.' Of course, I can't say that aloud."

To Rapaille, the Hummer SUV, based on the design of a military truck, was an embodiment of Social Darwinism, sending out a clear signal: "Don't mess with me because I can crush you." Geographer Stephen Graham sees the SUV as an expression of a "new urban militarism", which uses war as "the dominant metaphor in describing the perpetual and boundless condition of urban societies – at war against drugs, against crime, against terror, against insecurity itself". Instead of making roads safer for all motorists, you make them safer for the individual motorist by placing him inside a small tank. Indeed, sociological studies of SUV drivers show they exhibit more risky behaviour on the road, an "SUV effect", according to which drivers violate traffic lights, don't wear seat belts, and drive while using their mobile phones.

Behind the wheel of an XC90, I felt my primitive, reptilian instincts come alive. I was a winner, a conqueror, impregnable, stronger, bigger, faster, better. In short, I had become someone I used to despise. I was burning twice as much petrol as a Prius, and the car cost more than twice as much to buy. But wow, it felt great! And it didn't feel particularly Swedish, either. Indeed, the new XC90 emerged out of a tension between the Chinese and Swedish leaderships of Volvo. In 2013, Li publicly criticised Volvo's design, particularly interiors that he saw as "too Scandinavian". "In the beginning there were some misunderstandings – Li wanted to go luxury, Jacoby wanted to be Nordic," Sundemo recalls. Carl Peter Forster also noted this contrast:

"It is quite interesting to observe — to create a Swedish super-premium international brand entails some interesting challenges. One of the slight challenges we have is to present the premium-ness of Volvo in a country like China, where premium-ness is all to do with visual richness, gold plated things – which is absolutely un-Swedish. Lots of people love the restrained, minimal Swedish design using natural colours. For certain luxury brands that is difficult. Lots of Europeans have a soft spot for this refined luxury that has a sense of understatement and style. Not to the same extent in Asia or Russia."

The XC90 seems like an appropriate metaphor for the new Swedish model that emerged from the economic crisis of the 1990s. A victory of Swedish consensual manufacturing methods over cheap labour and orders from the top; and at the same time a victory for a Chinese entrepreneur's focus on a profitable market segment. A success for Swedish principles of safety, quality and style; yet also a triumph of hard-nosed marketing to a reptilian demographic that eschews modesty and demands luxury in spades.

197

From 2019, the XC90 will be available only as a hybrid that runs on both battery power and petrol. Similarly, the new Swedish model of the millennium's third decade will be a hybrid, a mix of pre-1990s industrial pragmatism with the globalised realities of the 21st century. The advertising slogan for Volvo cars is "Made By Sweden". It is now a feature of the new Swedishness that Volvo is no longer a Swedish company.

SUMMARY CHAPTER 7

What does the story of Volvo's XC90 tell us about the Swedish model today?

• Sweden is so open to international investment that it can stomach a takeover of one of its leading brands by an unknown Chinese company

• Geely succeeded where Ford – Volvo's previous owner – struggled because it allowed Volvo's Swedish managers and employees a great deal of freedom to do things the way they thought best

• The new Chinese owners injected much-needed entrepreneurial energy which Volvo lacked, making big and bold investments

198

• Their success relied on targeting a fast-growing global market segment

• Volvo's new SUV, the XC90, combines aspects of Sweden's historical preference for big, safe cars with the market's demand for luxury and status

• The XC90 is a handy metaphor for the new Swedish model, in which there is a productive tension between hard-nosed foreign ownership and a deep-rooted domestic manufacturing culture; between a market of wealthy customers and the traditions of Scandinavian personal restraint; between the need to meet individual needs and those of the broader collective; and between a product "made in Sweden" but dependent on a global market and parts from all over the world

CHAPTER 8

PAVED WITH GOOD INTENTIONS: SWEDEN'S ZERO CARBON PLAN

A tale of toxic exports; separating green gimmicks from climate fundamentals; the 2017 Climate Act; capitalism versus the environment; an experiment in green living; heating the people's home; but is it ambitious enough?

Sweden has a dirty little secret. For decades, it has been dumping dangerous toxic waste in a hole on a small island off the coast of Norway. That hole has rapidly filled up. The company that runs it started looking for somewhere else where it could put the toxins produced by Swedish power stations. It zeroed in on Brevik, a charming little village south of the capital, Oslo. For more than a century, the local cement factory had been digging limestone out of the rock underneath the town, creating 300 km of tunnels. These could now be stuffed with the nasty stuff.

Since the 1990s, Sweden has shipped the bulk of its toxic fly ash to the tiny Norwegian island of Langøya, just 50 km from Brevik, where it was mixed with noxious byproducts from Norway's paint industry and dumped in a huge pit. This had capacity for 10 million cubic meters, but by 2022 it would be full to overflowing. Noah, the company that runs the dump, looked at 100 sites across the country and narrowed it down to three, of which Brevik was the most attractive. Noah deals with waste from hundreds of industrial customers, mainly from Norway but also Sweden and Denmark. The company reckoned that, once Langøya was full, the Brevik dump would operate for 30 or 40 years.

Perhaps not surprisingly, the locals were not happy. From being an idyllic summer destination, Brevik would become known as toxic rubbish dump, they said. They cited expert opinion that the waste treatment plant nearby would be handling dangerous gasses and acid, just a few hundred meters from people's homes. The plan to dispose of this "cruel waste" in their back-yard should itself be thrown in the recycling bin, they said. At the time this book went to print, the debate was still in full swing.

It is ironic that Norway's little local difficulty should have arisen from a Swedish environmental success. After it banned putting waste into landfill rubbish dumps in 2005, Sweden burned increasing amounts of garbage, both household and industrial, generating heat and power while slashing green-house gas emissions. The process was so smooth and efficient that other countries paid to offload their waste onto Sweden – prompting awestruck speculation in foreign media that the country had "run out of rubbish" and was forced to import it. At one point in 2015, the country's 32 waste incineration plants needed nearly three times more trash than the country's households could provide.

Moreover, incineration was no longer controversial in Sweden, because it was clean. After Swedish scientists in the 1980s studied the release of diox-ins – dangerous mutagens and carcinogens – from municipal incinerators, strict requirements were introduced for cleaning up the process. The amount of waste burned for energy grew fourfold in 30 years, and the energy pro-duced went up six times, while total dioxin emissions fell by 99 per cent. Power companies boasted that their only emissions were water vapour. It was almost too good to be true. Like a small intestine for society, incinerators digested the detritus of modern life, extracting every last drop of usefulness and turning it into energy.

But the intestine still had to poop. And Sweden sent the poop to Norway, where it was causing problems. Yet the hype about Sweden's smart way of dealing with rubbish was immense. Here is well-known British entertainer James Corden on The Late Show on the US TV channel CBS:

Guys, this is going to blow your mind. In Sweden, they burn waste in gigan-tic, state-of-the-art recycling plants and use that energy for heat. It's really cool but there's one problem. They've run out of trash and they're having to import it from other countries. So to keep their economy running, they have to import trash. Sweden is amazing, it's incredible. The people are beautiful, they have no trash, nothing bad ever happens there. The worst thing to hap-pen to that entire country is when the band ABBA broke up.

You can almost hear him asking: "How does the bumblebee fly?!" But you don't need James Corden to tell you that, outside its borders, Sweden has an exceptionally good reputation on the environment. When you try to unpack the reasons for this, however, the question "Where's the poop?" keeps nagging away.

Part of the problem is untangling the measures that really make a difference from those that just sound nice, but are fluffy and ineffectual in the larger scheme of things. Janey Mehks is Stockholm's Business Development Manager for Cleantech. Cleantech, she explains, is any technology that is better for the environment than existing technology. "So everything, basically," she says. Mehks can point to all sorts of initiatives that come under the cleantech rubric – shared car services, green development zones, the world's first urban biochar carbon sink, urban agriculture, automated vacuum waste collection – but which of these are significant, and which are cute but not much more than good PR? Everything is presented as new, unique, innovative and sustainable, often with a slick YouTube video featuring a breathless voiceover, upbeat music and images of smiling children. But – where's the poop? Swedes are not genetically nicer or cleaner than any other people, yet when it comes to their greenness, one encounters a relentless and simplistic emphasis on the positive. "People's environmental awareness is higher here," says Mehks. "We are close to the archipelago and nature, people go into the countryside at the weekends." A group of foreign students in Stockholm in 2018 were treated to a boat tour of the archipelago with a speaker on "Sweden's interaction with nature and how that informs our business philosophy". Ugh.

In some respects, greenness comes easy for a country with no fossil fuel reserves, lots of wide open spaces and a temperate climate. More than half the energy Sweden generates is from renewable sources, of which the lion's share is hydropower. This puts it far ahead of the rest of the EU, although behind Norway and Iceland. Sweden also has abundant forests, creating a renewable supply of biomass as fuel. And it is cold up north, attracting energy-intensive industries such as data centres, who use the low ambient temperatures to cool their vast arrays of computers. In 2018, Facebook announced it would double the size of its date centres in Luleå, near the Arctic Circle, attracted by the cold, cheap prices for low-carbon hydro power, and tax breaks. At the time of the announcement, Facebook was already consuming more than one per cent of Sweden's total energy production, a proportion set to double with the expansion. Facebook is not alone – Stockholm receives inquiries from data centre companies almost every week, says Mekhs.

Sweden has also benefitted from some good timing and bold moves on the environment, helping to form its reputation as a world leader on this issue. In 1968, the Swedish government proposed that the United Nations hold its first summit on the environment, which it did in Stockholm in 1972, marking a turning point in global green politics and putting sustainability on the UN's agenda. The Stockholm Conference, as it came to be known, threw down a marker for the rest of the world. In 1991 Sweden became one of the first countries to tax carbon, gradually raising the levy to be the highest in the world. The tax has help the country cut greenhouse gas emissions by a quarter even while the economy has grown by 60 per cent – it has "decoupled" from emissions, to use the jargon. A tax on nitrogen oxide emissions from power plants, introduced in 1992, saw emissions decline by 50 per cent per unit of energy produced. In 2010, Stockholm became the first city to be named "the green capital of Europe", thanks to its efforts on noise pollution, cleaner water, waste disposal and open spaces. It gave the city a marketing boost, creating a new surge of attention in Sweden's green credentials.

At the UN's climate change conference in Paris in 2015, countries agreed to try to keep the increase in global average temperatures to below 2 degrees Celsius above pre-industrial levels. This spurred another eye-catching initiative in Stockholm, where left and right agreed that the country should aim to have zero carbon emissions by 2045. Shortly after the Paris agreement, Sweden became the first country to introduce legislation committing it to be "climate neutral" before the mid-point of the century. Stockholm, aimed to reach the target even earlier. The 2017 Climate Act, with its 2045 target, came about in part thanks to some of the features of the new Swedish model that we have encountered earlier. It is a benchmark against which we can measure the importance of some of the cuddly green initiatives taking place across the country. And it also raises the question of whether the Swedish bumblebee has hobbled itself with a new set of restrictions, making it harder to get off the ground.

AMBITIOUS ENOUGH?

First, there is a strong echo of the long-term outlook that we encountered in Chapter 3. Anders Wijkman, who chaired the committee of politicians and business leaders who came up with the 2045 target, says that Sweden's climate agreement breaks the pattern of short-termism in global economics:

"Since the 1980s, capitalism has moved from furthering the economic de-velopment of countries, regions and the world towards maximising profits, and then to a large extent profits from speculation. In addition, the cap-italism unleashed since 1980 in the Anglo-Saxon world, and since 1990 worldwide, is mainly financial, supported by excessive deregulation and liberalisation of the economy. The term 'shareholder value' popped up in the business pages of the media worldwide, as if that was now the new epiphany and guardrail for all economic action. In reality, it served to nar-row business down to short-term gains, often at the expense of social and ecological values."

Of course it would be silly to suggest there is direct link between the dual share structure of Swedish company ownership and the 2045 carbon goal. But Wijkman and politicians of left and right sat down to debate climate change with business leaders accustomed to thinking about the longer term, not just their next quarterly report. There were divisions among business lead-ers on climate issues, Wijkman says. But by including two business groups on the committee, they competed to out-do each other, neither wanting to be seen to be the bad guy.

205

Wijkman is also clear that short-term incentives are needed to reward long-term action. Not far to the north of Östermalm, Stockholm's posh central district, is an experiment in matching the short and long-term interests of construction companies, in an attempt to radically reduce carbon emissions from housing. The city administration is investing about €2 billion over 25 years to develop a former brown-field industrial site, used previously for gas and oil depots, which now enjoys the breathless title of the Royal Stockholm Seaport. This is a large-scale experiment in green city living. It has some fluffy stuff – like tunnels under the roads to prevent wandering frogs being crushed by SUVs. And it has some gimmicky, gee-whiz stuff – like a vacuum waste collection system, where all the bins are emptied automatically by vacuum suction several times a day. This at least has the benefit that the area needs fewer garbage trucks on its streets.

Most importantly, however, the city has imposed a strict limit on energy consumption for homes in this area – half the legal limit elsewhere in the city – and is making this progressively stricter while scoring all buildings on a range of sustainability measures, including longevity. When land is put out for tender, the better a company scores on these measures, the more chance it has of winning the contract. So far around 50 construction companies have signed up to these conditions and built apartment blocks in the area. In return they get to work with university research departments and high-tech companies to experiment with green urban design.

The homes are sold or rented out commercially, with prices around the same as any new apartments in central Stockholm – in other words, they are pricey. But there is a high demand for apartments in this location. All the same, because of the environmental requirements, companies don't make the same profits as they would elsewhere. It is a shop-window for them, and an opportunity to try out new design methods as legislation in Sweden, and Europe as a whole, continues to drive down energy consumption. "By learning how to build low energy buildings they are ahead of the competition, it is an investment for them," says Bo Hallqvist of the city development administration:

"Housing is a conservative business, money talks every minute – we are trying to change the business model here. As a municipality we own the planning process and use this power in the Royal Seaport. There is a lot of learning involved, learning to achieve less energy consumption, and to be

more robust. We have a 100-year perspective – these are not buildings that you will have to knock down in 40 years. Anyone can build a single block with high sustainability, but we are learning to do this on a large scale. When we can show we can build a lot of houses to this level of quality an environmental efficiency, then the city can decide to do the same across Stockholm. We are looking at what we can achieve for the long term."

As a result of this process, Stockholm has insisted that all new construction on land earmarked for development must now meet the energy consumption limits set by the Royal Stockholm Seaport. This level will be progressively reduced as the city nears its carbon-free goal in 2040.

Since the Seaport project began, political control over the city council has changed hands twice from left to right, and back again. But this has not affected progress, pointing to a second feature of the new Swedish model that we have encountered earlier in the book – the importance of consensus. Hallqvist says: "An important thing in Sweden is that we work with consensus all the time. We don't start major projects until all the major parties agree – we cannot afford for changes in political leadership to affect them." Wijkman describes this process at work on the committee that established the 2045 zero carbon target:

"In the climate debate neither the centre left or right bloc wanted the other to emerge as the more radical. There was an eagerness to agree that this is the type of issue that it is beneficial for society, but also for the parties themselves – to avoid constant bickering about targets and details. There were certain issues where I felt there was even an eagerness on the centre right and left to have a broad agreement, because they didn't want to be seen to be less ambitious than the other side."

One foreign company that appreciates the advantages of consensus on the environment is Northvolt, a start-up founded by two former executives of Tesla, the pioneer of electric cars in the US. Northvolt has plans to build Europe's largest factory for lithium-ion batteries, at a cost of $4bn, aiming to start large-scale production by 2020. The company was attracted to Sweden by clean, cheap energy, the proximity of key minerals in the Nordics, and the presence of academic expertise in battery production. But there was another aspect, according to Paolo Cerruti, Northvolt's Italian chief operating officer:

< Model of the future Royal Stockholm Seaport. The two left-of-central towers are brick gasometers built in the 1890s and now being transformed into sports and cultural venues

"THIS IS PROBABLY ONE OF THE EASIEST PLACES WHERE WE CAN DO IT, THEN WE CAN REPLICATE THAT MUCH MORE EASILY AROUND EUROPE."

Paolo Cerruti, *Northvolt's Italian chief operating officer*

208

"There was one more component which was very important. One of the major advantages of Sweden for doing business is the relative stability and common sense that politicians apply in this country. When administration B arrives in power, it will not scratch everything that administration A did, saying these guys are a bunch of jokers and this should never have happened – which is basically what the US did when Obama left power. This gives us a lot of confidence. If it is the right thing to do, they will support it, they will do it, regardless of who is in power. This gives visibility, stability, it is a pitch point for investors, especially non-Nordic investors."

For a company seeking to try out their concept and create a blueprint that could be replicated elsewhere, the local consensus on the environment helped it decide to build its first factory in Sweden. "This is probably one of the most entrepreneurship friendly places to get started, then we can replicate the same concept much more easily around Europe," Cerruti says. Strict environmental regulation and high wages were an entry barrier for Northvolt, he says, but setting the bar high in regulatory and cost terms forces companies to focus on efficiency and automation. This is another feature of the Swedish economy that we have encountered already in Chapter 2 – the system of relatively high wages forces companies to raise productivity by using the latest techniques, rather than driving down the price of labour. In the same way, a strict regulatory environment can be a spur for innovation, rather than just a drag on competitiveness.

Björn Hugosson, head of the climate unit at Stockholm's city hall, had a similar experience when he was tried to encourage greener transport in the city, by persuading private companies to use cars run on ethanol. He encountered surprisingly little resistance. "They wanted long-term rules" Hugosson says. "They said: If you provide us with the rules and strategy and tell us this will last for 20 years, as long as it is fair and is the same for anybody, then we can adapt." Stockholm has also converted a quarter of its busses to biogas, a byproduct of human sewage. In 2006 the Stockholm county administration agreed to buy all the biogas produced by the municipal water company for the next 20 years. This agreement between two public bodies helped to create the stable demand necessary to encourage private companies to step in and clean up the gas, making fuel for busses. The city has also developed a fleet of taxis running on ethanol and biogas.

Despite these successes, transport is a headache for Hugosson. Use of private cars is soaring in and around the capital, driven by trends in leisure and shopping. Moreover, neither the city's zero carbon target, nor the nation's, includes the vast amounts of carbon generated by manufacturing goods outside Sweden and transporting them into the country. The impact of consumption on the climate doesn't show up in the zero carbon calculation, even though in this respect a Swede is just as polluting as any other European citizen.

Where Stockholm, and other Swedish cities, have far more control is over their heating systems. District heating – where a central boiler supplies heat to many homes – spread rapidly in Sweden in the 1960s, consistent with a prevailing acceptance of centralised, community-wide solutions to social issues at the time. While centralised heating systems involve inevitable heat losses and big initial investments, there were also many advantages: cheap oil could be used to fire the boilers; large, centralised heating plants were efficient to maintain, and could also be used to generate cheap electricity – so-called combined heat and power; surplus heat from industry could be fed into the systems – everything from data centres to shops. Also, it was much easier to control emissions from a few large power plants than tens of thousands of local or domestic heating systems, leading to big improvements in air quality. About half of Sweden's homes are heated by district heating systems, and in Stockholm it is 80 per cent.

When concerns began to grow about greenhouse gas emissions, it was relatively easy to switch the district heating boilers to burn biomass and household or industrial waste. Crucially, the revenue from selling heat and power allowed operators to make a suitable profit, despite the high cost

210

of cleaning toxins from the emissions. District heating was an integral part of the folkhemmet – the people's home promised by the Swedish model in its earlier incarnation – and "one of the main reasons that Sweden performs so well on the environment", says Per-Oscar Hedman of Fortum, the Finnish energy company that jointly owns the Högdalen combined heat and power station in southern Stockholm, together with the city administration. Every few minutes, a huge truck rumbles through the gates, laden with waste destined for the furnaces – around 300 every day. When it was first built in 1970, Högdalen was well outside the city limits. But as the city expanded, so the power station has found itself surrounded by residential areas. Even on a sunny day, its huge chimney is not the neighbourhood's most beautiful feature, and 300 trucks heaped with garbage are not the nicest thing to have on the roads. But the generator does not incite fear or opposition, because it is clean. Ending toxic exports to Norway, however, will mean moving away from incineration towards much more thorough-going changes in production methods and recycling.

Stockholm city maintains a 50 per cent stake in the heating side of Fortum. For Hugusson, this is an important factor in the city's goal to become carbon free by 2040: "The lesson is that if you have a system you control, you can take measures to phase out emissions," he says. "When power stations are in the hands of private owners, you can't." A similar point is made by Oskar Larsson of the climate department at the Swedish Environmental Protection Agency, who says partnerships between the public and private sectors are necessary when large and risky investments need to be made, such as carbon capture and storage technologies. "If we want that to happen, government has to team up with industry – it will cost tax payers' money at the beginning," Larsson says. He also points to a collaboration between a private Swedish steel company, a publicly owned iron ore miner and a public utility, backed by the state, to develop a zero-emissions method for making steel. Called Hybrit, this project – if successful – could revolutionise steel production world-wide and slash Sweden's total carbon emissions by 10 per cent.

In short, a history of bold political initiatives, a consensus culture, a long-term outlook and suspicion of short-termism, centralised heating systems, municipal intervention and partnerships with the private sector have all combined to create conditions in which Sweden could commit to going carbon neutral by 2045, and have a chance of actually doing so. Whether or not this is enough, however, is quite another question. "Zero emissions" does not mean that in 2045 Sweden won't emit any greenhouse gases – the Climate Act commits the country to reduce its absolute emissions by 85

per cent below the level it had back in 1990. It plans to offset its remaining emissions by investing in projects that contribute to reducing pollution elsewhere. Also, as we have already seen, the calculation doesn't include the production and transport of products from abroad. And doesn't the rich world deserve to take a larger share of the burden of carbon reduction, because it has been irresponsibly affluent for so long?

Taking these factors into account, Wijkman says, Sweden's emissions target should be at least twice as ambitious. A transformation of capitalism on that scale has barely begun, he says: "Even if our proposals can be as relatively ambitious, they are not ambitious enough." There is one other way in which Sweden is better prepared than other countries to tackle the problem, however. Any such transformation will create losers, companies, industries and even entire sectors that will have to be closed down. How so-called "stranded assets" like this are dealt with is an issue largely neglected by climate policy makers. Sweden's transition system, which we looked at in Chapter 2, makes the country better equipped than most to cope with closing down parts of the economy that are an obstacle to achieving climate objectives.

Inside Sweden's Environmental Protection Agency, Hans Wrådhe looks like the very essence of an environmental scientist – a warm and friendly face, earnest spectacles, and a T-shirt from a holiday to Dubrovnik that looks like it took place several years ago. Wrådhe is responsible for checking Sweden's progress towards hitting its green targets. Does Sweden deserve its reputation as a front-runner on climate change and the environment? Wrådhe says:

213

"Sweden is special in that we are the first country that has a Climate Act and a clear goal to become climate neutral. But in terms of consumption, we are not an ideal country. We have quite a lot to do ourselves before we tell others to be better."

< The Högdalen power station in southern Stockholm, which burns 750,000 tonnes of domestic and industrial waste a year to generate both power and heat for the district's homes

SUMMARY CHAPTER 8

To sum up: is the Swedish bumblebee nimble enough to go green enough, fast enough? The following aspects of the new Swedish model have combined to encourage Sweden to declare it will go carbon neutral by 2045:

• A history of taking bold, well-timed political initiatives, with business on board

• A familiarity with putting long-term priorities above short-term commercial interests

• A tradition of political consensus, creating the stability necessary for long term investment decisions

• The "people's home" approach in the 1960s led to investment in extensive district heating systems, which have been very amenable to climate goals

• Sweden's transition system, with its job security agencies, makes it easier to close down unwanted industries

• There is a tradition of the public sector working with the private sector on problems that require large and risky investments up front.

CONCLUSION: THE NEW SWEDISH MODEL

When I moved to Sweden, I swapped a small apartment in London for a house with a garden. It has a rhododendron bush, which blooms first with white flowers in May, followed shortly by an eruption of purple. The bush is a magnet for insects, particularly bumblebees, who occasionally stray into the kitchen and need to be coaxed back into the sunlight. The long cold Swedish winter gives the bees a short time to build their nests, rear their offspring and collect stores of honey before they hibernate, so they work at high speed. Heaven knows where they all come from; bumblebee nests are notoriously hard to find. Charles Darwin gave his children sugar sprinklers filled with flour, so they could shake it onto passing bumblebees and help their father spot their flight paths. Since then, a small army of mellitologists have spent hours sitting in fields, gardens and laboratories, patiently watching and measuring.

Although much more is known about these insects than in Darwin's time, for decades their flight remained an enigma. In 1934, a French zoologist and engineer, Antoine Magnan, and his assistant André Sainte-Laguë examined bees and calculated definitively that *"leur vol est impossible"* – their flight is impossible. It took another 70 years for scientists in California to crack the secret. Into a tank filled with two tons of oil they placed a pair of mechanical wings 60 cm across, driven by computer-controlled motors. The wings stirred the fluid and created currents that could be observed thanks to a stream of air bubbles injected into the tank. The set-up was illuminated by rays of laser light and filmed by video cameras, while sensors recorded the forces exerted on the wings. This mechanical insect, imitating the movements of wings at a speed 1,000 times slower and on a scale 100 times greater, enabled the scientists to reveal how the bee uses a vortex of air around its wings to generate sufficient lift. The key to apian flight turned out to be a low-amplitude, high frequency wingbeat, at more than 200 beats per second. At Harvard, scientists have now created a "robobee", measuring half the size of a paper clip and weighing less that one-tenth of a gramme, that flies by mimicking the insect.

Another myth destroyed by science is that bumblebee flight is a rather hither-and-thither, random and impetuous affair. This motion is captured wonderfully by Nikolai Rimsky-Korsakov in his glittering, three-minute operatic interlude, which he wrote in 1899 to evoke how a magic swan princess changed a young man into an insect so that he could fly away to visit the tsar – proof, if any was needed, that utterly insane plot lines can still inspire the most sublime music (although to be fair, he also had Pushkin's sublime poetry to be inspired by). But we now know that Rimsky-Korsakov was technically incorrect: the flight of the bumblebee is extremely logical and coherent. The energy required to lift its body off the ground is considerable, so it needs to eat frequently to keep flying. A human being consumes the calories contained in a Mars Bar by running for about an hour. Were there to be such a thing as a human-sized bumblebee, it would burn off the same calories in 30 seconds. Any unnecessary buzzing about is therefore potentially fatal to a bumblebee. If you find one crawling miserably on the ground, it has probably just run out of energy; you must let it sip on some sugar syrup to get it going again.

As a result, bumblebee flight is remarkably efficient. The insects have evolved a means of detecting the time elapsed since a flower was visited by another bee. If this is less than the time taken for the flower's stamen to fill with nectar once more after being drained by the previous visitor, the bumblebee will move to a different flower, so as not to waste energy on an empty bloom. Moreover, different flowers preferred by the bee take different times to refill with nectar, so bumblebees have also learned to make allowance for the species of flower. This efficiency means that bumblebees can fly even when laden with their own bodyweight of pollen and nectar. Indeed, far from being a freak that somehow manages to fly – bumbling about, as its name suggests – the bumblebee is in fact an aerodynamic superstar. It is a Zeppelin of the insect world, formidably muscular and lean.

Which brings us to our Swedish bumblebee. No metaphor is perfect, and I know I am in danger of stretching this particular one too far. But in the previous chapters we have seen that Sweden's economy has several distinctive features which, in the eyes of an outsider, might suggest that it should not

217

fly. And yet, not only does it does so adequately enough, in fact it flies better than might be expected, all things considered. So let us try to sum up what we have learned.

There is a new Swedish model. It is not particularly "new", in the sense that it emerged from the economic wreckage of the 1990s and so has been around for a while. But it is new in the sense that most people's opinions of it need updating. Also, the past two decades have served to demonstrate a basic characteristic: the new model is a shared creature of both left and right. It is no longer true to say that the Swedish model is "social democratic" – and keen-eyed business and the conservative centre right are more than content to espouse its key features. An important aspect is centralised wage bargaining, where the international competitiveness of Sweden's main export industries sets the benchmark for all sectors. This in turn keeps the wages structure relatively flat and high, forcing industry to innovate or die. This aspect of the "old" 1960s model fell apart in the 80s but was resurrected in the late 90s. In turn, it depends upon a tradition of mutual trust forged in the 1930s, in which trade unions acquiesce in the need for constant upheaval and change, while employers take some responsibility for the consequences of restructuring for workers.

Another feature of the model is the apparent dominance of investors with a long-term view of business, hardwired into their outlook through the system of dual shares. Corporate power lies not with management but with shareholders who are obliged to take part in big, strategic decisions. Instead of anonymous investment funds or small investors focused on making a quick buck, there are strong owners with a name, a responsibility, and a clear role. This approach is combined with a management style that emphasises consensus and involvement. It may be cumbersome at times, but it helps give consistency to business decisions, and encourages initiative. These factors have helped a small country create some of the biggest names in global industry. In the second decade of the millennium, they also combined to create a highly creative entrepreneurial environment, turning Stockholm into one of the hottest locations for high-tech startups. The rise of companies such as Spotify, Skype, iZettle and Klarna have fuelled talk of a "Nordic silicon valley". Sweden has also become a very open country, welcoming foreign investment in some of its flagship companies.

The model, old and new, has made it a priority to help women combine work with having a family. To weaken the tendency for women to take on a double burden of domestic and professional work, Sweden has used carrots and sticks to encourage men to share the burden of childcare. Starting in

218

the 1960s from a need to fill a gaping hole in the workforce, Swedish family policy was also driven by the notion that sex discrimination is economically inefficient. Today it has acquired a further justification, with governments of left and right espousing feminism as part of a wider ambition to be a beacon for humanitarianism and human rights. In turn, this attitude has fostered an openness to asylum and immigration, though this is being tested by the most recent influx of refugees from man-made catastrophes in Syria, Iraq, Afghanistan and the Horn of Africa. The model has gained a reputation for being environmentally conscious, and aspects of Swedish capitalism would indeed appear to lend themselves to the vision, ambition and organisation necessary to effect a green transformation of industry and society. But it is too early to say whether the country's latest mission to become carbon neutral by 2045 is more than a green gloss on a problem that requires more fundamental change.

Sweden is living proof that regulated capitalism can be highly effective and sustainable, and that the state can play a useful role. This is a society that, on the one hand, adheres to the principles of a market economy, including competition, free trade, openness and innovation. On the other hand, it does not suffer from a naive belief that markets are self-regulatory and that politics should be all about de-regulation, tax cuts and paring back the state. It is based on an understanding that, in order to work well in creating human welfare, the market economy needs a fairly extensive public system of regulation. Moreover, the new Swedish model has been championed in Sweden by both centre left and centre right governments during the past two decades – there is plenty of room for debate over emphasis and direction, but there is agreement over the underlying parameters. Emmanuel Macron, the French president who championed a "third way" between right and left made much of the Nordic model as a providing solutions for France. The impeccably free-market Economist magazine has proclaimed that the Nordics, Sweden included, are "the next supermodel", countries that have "reached the future first" and are offering "highly innovative solutions that reject the tired orthodoxies of left and right".

The term "model" is a retrospective construction, and there is a tendency to see it as an empty bottle into which you can pour any wine of your choice. For Maria Rankka, for example, until recently the CEO of the Stockholm Chamber of Commerce and formerly head of Sweden's leading free market think tank, Timbro, a key element of the Swedish model is "its ability to re-invent itself". Far from being fixed, its capacity for constant change is its very essence, she says:

"PEOPLE TEND TO HAVE STRONG OPINIONS ABOUT SWEDEN, THEY EITHER LIKE IT OR HATE IT. AND WHICHEVER IT IS, PEOPLE TEND TO HAVE EXAGGERATED VIEWS. PEOPLE WHO LOVE IT ARE MISINFORMED, AND THOSE WHO HATE IT ARE MISINFORMED."

Maria Rankka, *recently CEO of the Stockholm Chamber of Commerce*

"My interpretation of the Swedish model is quite different from that of the Social Democrats, but it is a good brand name. It's like the first Obama presidential campaign slogan – 'change'. You could project whatever you wanted onto the word, it was quite abstract. It is the same with the Swedish model. For the centre left I guess it is all about trade unions and negotiation."

I encountered this point of view on several occasions during interviews for this book, but based on the evidence gathered here I would beg to differ. Yes, the Swedish model is undoubtedly a good brand name, and yes, here are clearly different interpretations of what is fundamental to it. But there is something more substantial here, aspects of an economy that are real and effable and distinctive. The fact that important features of the model fell apart in the 1980s and were pieced back together again helps us to see their significance today in sharper outline. We are dealing with a bumblebee here, not a butterfly or a daddy longlegs. But nobody has thought to catalogue the bumblebee's attributes for a while, so they seem to have become somewhat obscured or forgotten. It is time to get out the sugar sprinkler and get shaking.

The new Swedish model is not the same as the 1970s version. Sweden has accepted fiscal discipline – a low inflation target, balanced budgets, limited deficits – partly imposed by membership of the European Union, and partly a response to the perceived profligacy of the 1980s. The central bank has been independent of government since 1999. Large chunks of the public sec-

tor are now in private hands. Foreign companies can purchase Swedish businesses, even the big ones. Wealth and inheritance taxes have been scrapped, and rates of taxation are nothing out of the ordinary. Swedish attitudes have changed, too. When asked what the Swedish model stood for in 2012, Swedes put tax-funded schools and welfare in first place, unsurprisingly – generous welfare is quintessentially Swedish. More unexpected was the answer that came in second place: "Everyone has the right to choose schools and health-care centres". These sorts of choices were nowhere to be seen 40 years ago.

As an economy, Sweden looks much more like the rest of the world today than it did back then. And yet it *is* different (see Chapters 1 to 8 above). If it wasn't different, surely it wouldn't provoke such passionate views for and against. Rankka is right when she points out that Sweden tends to be like Kalles Kaviar, that strange, pale-pink, salt-sweet cod roe concoction that Swede's squeeze out of a toothpaste tube onto their eggs in the morning, and which is either loved or loathed. "People tend to have strong opinions about Sweden, they either like it or hate it. And whichever it is, people tend to have exaggerated views. People who love it are misinformed, and those who hate it are misinformed," she says.

Criticising Sweden used to be a minority sport enjoyed by conservative economists eager to prove that anything but the unregulated free market leads to inefficiency and decline. But since Donald Trump's ascendancy in the US, the ranks of detractors have been swelled by people who want to see Sweden fail. The country is identified in the minds of liberals and conservatives alike as some sort of progressive paradise, polarising attitudes towards Sweden and giving supporters of a socially conservative world view a target: get Sweden, and the liberals will have nothing to hold onto, they reason. This book has tried to spell out that there is much more to the Swedish model than liberal attitudes. This is modern welfare capitalism, and – for now, at least – it is functioning relatively well according to standard measures of success for capitalist economies. Perhaps the detractors will provoke Swedes to put up a better defence of what they have achieved, and how they have done it. This is the view of Natalia Brzezinski, chief executive of Brilliant Minds, an annual conference in Stockholm backed by some of Sweden's leading business figures. She says:

"People are talking about the Swedish model now, they are realising there is something special to be proud of, but it has all been hidden. The tech people have done a lot, they have made Swedes proud. This country is a symbol of what can be done, there should be a coming out party for the Swedish model – it has been a sleepy place for so long."

222

How long can the party continue? Some might see a threat to the model from the recent rise of right-wing populists who combine opposition to immigration with visceral prejudice against Islam. Certainly the arrival of this brand of right-wing politics in or close to government would deliver a blow to Sweden's image abroad. At the time of writing, in Norway and Finland far-right parties currently enjoy ministerial positions, while in Denmark their support keeps a minority centre-right administration in power. There is nothing exceptional about Sweden that would prevent its politics from going in similar directions. But as far as image is concerned, Sweden may not have so much to fear. It surprises me that Denmark, which long ago jettisoned any pretence of social liberalism, still enjoys such a cuddly image abroad associated with *hygge* and *lykke*, when it is so clearly *hygge* for some, but not for asylum seekers and refugees.

The inroads made by populists are a sign that all is not as well with the model as might be assumed. Significant numbers of people feel left out. This book presents a top-down view of Swedish society, from people for whom life is comfortable and the model is working fine. Looked at from below, most Swedes lead busy, hard-working lives holding down jobs and raising families; margins are tight, and some find it more of a struggle than others. If the economy fails to deliver for them, then they will look for alternatives on the left and the right. But as this book shows, the Swedish model is about much more than politics. Further successes for populists would challenge the fundamentals, but not erase them – the underlying features of the model are likely to be around for a while to come.

Sweden's high dependence on the world economy makes it vulnerable to the vagaries of capitalism beyond its borders. But it came through the 2008 crash better than most, and has built buffers against future crises. In Soviet times, Russians used to joke: why is western capitalism on the edge of a precipice? Answer: so they can get a better look at us down here. That rather sums up Sweden's position relative to a systemic crisis. This society has problems like any other, but they are not on a scale likely to bring the bumblebee crashing down any time soon. The challenge, in the meantime, is surely to make the new Swedish model work better for more people.

223

SOURCES

Introduction: And Yet it Flies
My *Guardian* article that appears to have started the Chinese whispers: David Crouch, "Efficiency up, turnover down: Sweden experiments with six-hour working day", theguardian.com, September 17, 2015

You can find all the quotes from other newspapers on news aggregating sites such as Factiva. Here is the *New York Times* article: Liz Alderman, "In Sweden, an Experiment Turns Shorter Workdays Into Bigger Gains", NYTimes.com, May 20, 2016

That viral Facebook video: www.facebook.com/enjoy.science/videos/329209404093610/

The bumblebee quote by Göran Persson is taken from his opening address to a conference of Sweden's Social Democratic Party in Stockholm on March 10, 2000, and is quoted in Subhash Thakur et al, Sweden's Welfare State: Can the Bumblebee Keep Flying? International Monetary Fund, Washington DC, 2003

Chapter 1: 'Less Blood, Sweat and Tears'
Lagom – a uniquely Swedish word meaning neither too much nor too little, but just enough, everything in moderation

Karl Olov Arnstberg's opinions on Swedishness: "Are Swedes really tall, blonde and blue-eyed?" Sveriges Radio, July 12, 2014

Frantzén quote: Johan Ronge, "Fackets hårda krav mot Sveriges rikaste kvinna", expressen.se, Feb 22, 2018

For a good summary of the early decades of Swedish labour relations, see Anders Kjellberg, "The Swedish Model of Industrial Relations: Self-Regulation and Combined Centralisation-Decentralisation," in Craig Phelan (ed.), *Trade Unionism since 1945: Towards a Global History, Vol 1*, 2009, p.155–198

Bedrock of the Swedish model: Richard Milne, "Global threat fails to break spirit of Sweden's labour model," FT.com, Jan 6, 2014

TCO video about Joe Williams, by PR Bureau ANR BBDO: vimeo.com/84733222

TCO "Business like a Swede" video, also by PR Bureau ANR BBDO: www.youtube.com/watch?v=OcVoKPTS7AU

The second most shared video on YouTube in its first 24 hours... Angelica Rylin, "Storytelling – Like a Swede", angelica.themurderofmysweet.com, Oct 13, 2014

Labour Policy Council survey of business attitudes to the unions: Hur Fungerar Kollektivavtalen? Arbetsmarknadsekonomiska rådet, Stockholm, 2018

"A flat corporate structure is a logical and cost-efficient way to operate..." Pär Isaksson, Leading Companies in a Global Age – Managing the Swedish Way. Stockholm, VINNOVA Swedish Governmental Agency for Innovation Systems, 2008

For more on the "Swedish management style", see: Bjursell, C., Transformative leadership: A Swedish case. In: Daphne Halkias, Joseph C. Santora, Nicholas Harkiolakis, Paul W. Thurman (eds.), Leadership and Change Management: A Cross-Cultural Perspective. Routledge, 2017, pp114–119; Fredrik Movitz and Åke Sandberg, "All Gone but Still There: The Swedish Model and Swedish Management. On Scandinavian Perspectives on Management in Swedish Working Life," Department of Sociology, University of Stockholm, 2011; Tor Grenness, "Will the 'Scandinavian leadership model' survive the forces of globalisation? A SWOT analysis", International Journal of Business and Globalisation 7(3), 2011, 332–350; Holmberg, I. and Åkerblom, S. "Primus Inter Pares – Leadership and Culture in Sweden", in Chokar, J. S. et al (eds.) Culture and Leadership Across the World: The GLOBE Book of In-Depth Studies of 25 Societies. New Jersey, Lawrence Erlbaum Associates, 2007; Bengt Gustavsson, "Human values in Swedish management," Journal of Human Values, 1, 1995, 153–71.

Chapter 2: Sweden's Hidden Welfare System

When I was researching this book, I began to feel that I had made a genuine discovery in revealing the hidden welfare system in Sweden that helps people change jobs. So little had been written about it elsewhere, even in Swedish. But then Alana Semuels, a staff writer for the Atlantic magazine in New York, wrote a brilliant piece about Sweden's job security agencies, asking: "What If Getting Laid Off Wasn't Something to Be Afraid Of?" theatlantic.com, October 25, 2017. The New York Times did an interesting "follow" a couple of months later: Peter S. Goodman, "The Robots Are Coming, and Sweden Is Fine", NYTimes.com, December 27, 2017. The OECD issued a report on the system in 2015, entitled *Back to Work: Sweden – Improving the Re-employment Prospects of Displaced Workers*.

To protect her privacy, Gunilla Stensson is not her real name, but she is a very real person.

"As Meidner himself put it many years later..." Meidner quoted by Mark Blyth, "The transformation of the Swedish model," *World Politics*, 54, October 2001, pp1–26. (The original quote is from a book dated 1984, which I have not read.)

LO's attitude to globalisation and structural transformation as "opportunities rather than threats": Thomas Carlén, *Inequality is Bad for Business – A Progressive Agenda for Equality*. LO, Report to the World Economic Forum, Davos, 2017

86 per cent of Swedes agree with the statement that "globalisation is an opportunity for economic growth": Eurobarometer, "Designing Europe's Future: Trust in Institutions, Globalisation, Support for the Euro, Opinions About Free Trade and Solidarity", *Special Eurobarometer 461*, European Union, 2017

A remarkably flat society in terms of earned income... That and the following paragraph are based on Douglas A. Hibbs Jr. and Håkan Locking, "Wage Dispersion and Productive Efficiency: Evidence for Sweden," *Journal of Labor Economics* 18, no. 4 (October 2000): 755–782

"Full-blown confrontation regime..." Nils Elvander, "Industrivatalet och Saltsjöbadsavtalet – en jämförelse", *Arbetsmarknad & Arbetsliv* 8 (3), 2002, pp191–204

Public debt doubled... Pär Nuder, Saving the Swedish Model, Institute for Public Policy Research, London, 2012

Medineo's remark that "The Swedish system, balancing private ownership and social control, has broken down." Rudolph Meidner, "Why Did the Swedish Model Fail?" *Socialist Register*, 1993, 211–228

The original text of the Industry Agreement is also available in English: "Agreement on industrial development and wage formation", Almega, 1997, and can be found here: www.industriradet.se

The economic history sections of this chapter also draw on the following sources: Interview with Per Ewaldsson, senior legal advisor, Medlingsinstitutet; Kristina Ahlen, "Swedish Collective Bargaining Under Pressure", *British Journal of Industrial Relations* 27:3, November, 1989, pp330–346; Dominique Anxo and Harald Niklasson, The Swedish Model: Revival After the Turbulent 1990s? *ILO Discussion Paper*, 200; Andreas Bergh, "On the Rise, Fall and Revival of a Capitalist Welfare State", *New Political Economy*, Volume 19, Issue 5, 2014, pp662–694; Thomas Carlén, "Adapting the Nordic Model", in David Coates (ed.), *Exiting from the Crisis*, 2011, pp189–195; Lennart Erixon, "The Rehn-Meidner Model in Sweden: Its Rise, Challenges and Survival", *Journal of Economic Issues* Volume 44, Issue 3, 2010, pp677–715; Lennart Erixon, "The Rehn–Meidner model's relation to contemporary economics and the Stockholm School", *The European Journal of the History of Economic Thought*, Volume 18, 2011, issue 1, pp85–123; Johannes Lindvall, "Vad hände med den aktiva arbets-marknadspolitiken?", *Ekonomisk Debatt*, volym 39, nummer 3, 2011, pp38–45; Juhana Vartiainen, To Create and Share – The Remarkable Success and Contested Future of the Nordic Social-Democratic Model. *FAFO*, 2014; Juhana Vartiainen, "Nordic Collective Agreements", in Lars Mjøset (ed.), *The Nordic Varieties of Capitalism*, 2015, pp331–363; Ilya Viktorov, "The Swedish Employers and the Wage-Earner Funds Debate during the Crisis of Fordism in the 1970s and 1980s", *Conference Paper*, Stockholm University, Department of Economic History, 2009

Lars Walter's book on the job security agencies is Walter (ed.), *Mellan jobb. Omställningsavtal och stöd till uppsagda i Sverige*, Stockholm, SNS Förlag, 2015

The quote from Niklas Adalberth is taken from a 2015 interview I did with him for the *Financial Times*: David Crouch, "Klarna: payments company lets customers try before they pay", FT.com, June 5, 2015

Silicon valley seems oblivious to the value of experience... Hannah Kuchler, "No country for middle-aged techies", FT.com, April 28, 2017

The OECD stats on Swedish skill levels are in *Skills Outlook 2017*: Skills and Global Value Chains, OECD, 2017

Chapter 3: 'The 100 Year Plan'
Canadian scepticism about Haparanda: Minutes of the Standing Committee on Foreign Affairs and International Development, House of Commons, Canada, November 20, 2012

Some general background to the Haparanda IKEA deal: David Carr, "Det hemliga spelet om Ikea", nsd.se, September 27, 2016

Kamprad's "jungle capitalism" quote: "Ingvar Kamprad ser en ny sorts marknadsekonomi", svd.se, December 12, 2005

"We fell in love..." Torkel Omnell, "Dokument: Buchts kamp för Ikea", nsd.se, November 15, 2006

On the "Anglo-Saxon model", see the succinct definition given by Gideon Rachman, chief foreign affairs columnist at the *Financial Times*: "Definition of Anglo-Saxon capitalism", lexicon. ft.com (no date)

Richard Twomey, "Sweden, you have got to be joking..." Quoted by Richard Milne, "Meet the Wallenbergs", FT.com, June 15, 2015

On dual shares, Facebook and Google: Andrea Tan and Benjamin Robertson, "Why Investors Are Fretting Over Dual-Class Shares", bloomberg. com, July 10, 2017

On dual shares in Sweden, see for example, "Our company right or wrong", economist.com, March 15, 2007

Fredrik Lundberg's rare interview with the *Financial Times*: Richard Milne, "Sweden's new business king takes the long-term view", FT.com, January 5, 2015. Lundberg declined to be interviewed for this book.

The Swedish economy is increasingly owned from abroad: foreign ownership on the Stockholm stock exchange rose from 8 per cent in 1991 to 41 per cent in 2017. Of what is left, 15 Swedish families control 70 percent. In 2017, the 15 largest business families managed companies worth €480 billion (by comparison, Sweden's

total economic output in the same year was €440 billion). The Wallenberg family controls companies valued at almost €19 billion. See Majsa Allelin et al, "Ägande- och förmögenhetsstrukturen och dess förändring sedan 1980", *Katalys 55*, 2018, 3–35

"This is not how it works in Sweden..." Pär Karlsson, "M-ledaren sågar Östling för skatteuttalande", aftonbladet.se, November 7, 2017

"Royalty that celebrates its privileges..." PM Nilsson, "De rika och legitimiteten", di.se, January 26, 2015

I took a brief look at Swedish attitudes to the monarchy for the *Guardian*: David Crouch, "Sweden gears up for royal wedding as republican sentiments rise," theguardian.com, June 12, 2015

Quotes from experts on inequality in Sweden are taken from research I did for a *Guardian* article: David Crouch, "The new 'people's home': how Sweden is waging war on inequality", theguardian.com, July 17, 2017. Some quotes are from the article itself.

The source of Per Molander's remark about the rapid increase of inequality in Sweden can be found in OECD documents, such as "OECD Income inequality data update: Sweden (January 2015)", which states that the growth in inequality in Sweden between 1985 and the early 2010s was the largest among all OECD countries, increasing by one third.

Angel Gurria is quoted in "Inequality hurts economic growth, finds OECD research", oecd.org, December 9, 2014

On the IMF, see for example: Prakash Loungani and Jonathan D. Ostry, "The IMF's Work on Inequality: Bridging Research and Reality", blogs.imf. org, February 22, 2017; Angela Gaviria, "Response to Article: 'The IMF is Showing Some Hypocrisy on Inequality'", imf.org, February 16, 2017.

Chapter 4: Absolutely VABulous
"In order that women shall be emancipated from their antiquated role..." Olof Palme, "The Emancipation of Man", address to the Women's National Democratic Club, Washington D.C., June 8, 1970

"We have to expand society's facilities for childcare..." Olof Palme, speech at the UN Conference of International Women's Year, Mexico City, June 23, 1975

In the 1950s, Sweden had a lower participation rate of women in the workforce than Britain... Mary Ruggie, *The State and Working Women: A Comparative Study of Britain and Sweden*. Princeton University Press, 1984, p144

The number of publicly provided childcare spaces increased rapidly... Kimberly Earles, "Swedish Family Policy – Continuity and Change in the Nordic Welfare State", *Social Policy & Administration* Vol. 45, No. 2, 2011, pp180–193

Simultaneously, the amount of paid time off for parents... Ann-Zofie Duvander, "Svensk föräldraförsäkrings utveckling och konsekvenser", *Søkelys på arbeidslivet* Vol. 34, No. 01–02, 2017, pp126–143

That internet forum discussing the situation for Swedish women abroad: http://www.familjeliv. se/forum/thread/57154370-barnomsorg-utom-lands

The number of fathers taking paternity leave had stalled... Katrin Bennhold, "In Sweden, Men Can Have It All," NYTimes.com, June 9, 2010

"The lack of gender equality is not only an injustice..." Bengt Westerberg and others, "Ökad jämställdhet: Motion till riksdagen 1985/86:A604", January 27, 1986

"I always thought if we made it easier for women to work..." Westerberg interviewed by Bennhold, see above.

Subsidised childcare places expanded to nearly 730,000 by 2002. The figure is cited by Earles, see above.

Fathers take around a quarter of the total parental leave on average... Duvander, see above. Sweden spends four times as much of its wealth on early childhood education and care than the United States... Claudia Olivetti and Barbara Petrongolo, "The Economic Consequences of Family Policies: Lessons from a Century of Legislation in High-Income Countries," *Journal of Economic Perspectives*, Vol. 31, No.1, 2017, pp205–230

Despite the economic crisis of the early 1990s, Sweden still managed to expand its system of childcare... Sweden is not alone in this respect. A study by the OECD found that, in an era of perceived permanent austerity and overall welfare state retrenchment, rich countries have not been prevented from expanding family policies.

Emanuele Ferragina and Martin Seeleib-Kaiser, "Determinants of a Silent (R)evolution: Understanding the Expansion of Family Policy in Rich OECD Countries", *Social Politics*, Vol. 22, No. 1, 2014, pp1–37

On the Sweden Democrats and women's equality, see Diana Mulinari Anders Neergaard, "Doing Racism, Performing Femininity: Women in the Sweden Democrats", in Michaela Köttig et al (eds), *Gender and Far Right Politics in Europe*, e-book, Palsgrave, 2017, pp13–27

Hwang and Haas reported a dramatic increase in corporate support in large Swedish companies for fathers taking leave... Linda Haas and C. Philip Hwang, "Is Fatherhood Becoming More Visible at Work? Trends in Corporate Support for Fathers Taking Parental Leave in Sweden," *Fathering*, Vol. 7, No. 3, 2009, pp303–321

"The male norm of full-time employment remains strong..." C. Philip Hwang, "Even when fathers take lots of parental leave, mothers end up with more responsibility for childcare. Why?" https://fatherhood.global, May 31, 2016

Swedish women experience a large drop in relative earnings... See, for example, Nikolay Angelov et al, "Parenthood and the Gender Gap in Pay", *Journal of Labor Economics*, Vol. 34, no. 3, 2016, pp545–579; James Albrecht et al, "Parental Leave and the Glass Ceiling in Sweden", presentation at the European Society of Population Economics in Braga, Portugal, June 2014

Chapter 5: The Challenge of Immigration
"Spending more of the nation's income on foreign aid than any other country in 2015." According to the OECD's statistics here: https:// data.oecd.org/oda/net-oda.htm

"Maybe I should change his name..." The quote is from Martin Sandbu and David Crouch, "Riots in Sweden: Fire in the people's home", FT.com, May 24, 2013. On grievances against racism and the police, see David Couch, "Stockholm violence exposes grievances against the police", FT.com, May 23, 2013

Reinfeldt's "open your hearts" speech was widely reported. His remarks about Sweden having "more space than you can imagine" are less well known: Hanna Jakobson, "Fredrik Reinfeldt: Gott om plats för flyktingar", expressen.se, December 7, 2014

227

"My Europe doesn't build walls..." Tal av stats-minister Stefan Löfven vid manifestationen för flyktingar, Medborgarplatsen, Stockholm, den 6 september 2015, regeringen.se

"It pains me that Sweden is no longer capable of receiving asylum seekers..." Quoted in David Crouch, "Sweden slams shut its open-door policy towards refugees", theguardian.com, November 24, 2015

The country was set up as a whipping boy for multiculturalism... In the first six months of 2017, far-right website Breitbart published well over 100 articles claiming that immigration was wreaking havoc in Sweden (Paul Rapacioli, *Good Sweden, Bad Sweden: The Use and Abuse of Swedish Values in a Post Truth World*, Stockholm, Volante, 2018, p56). Britain's *Daily Mail* was not far behind in conducting an orchestrated campaign against Sweden's asylum policy. The racist message was relentless – "black people are violent criminals". At the time of writing (May, 2018), this crude message continues to be pumped out from an unholy alliance of Alt Right websites and Kremlin-backed organisations such as Russia Today and Sputnik.

Slashing immigrants with a samurai sword... David Crouch, "Sweden school attack: police treat killing of pupil and teacher as racist hate crime," theguardian.com, October 23, 2015

My report from Rosengård: David Crouch, "Grenade attacks shock Swedish city". FT.com, August 23, 2015

More than half the total unemployed would consist of people born outside the country... At the end of 2016, 335,000 people were unemployed in Sweden, of whom 160,000 – or 48 per cent – were foreign born. Arbetsmarknadssituationen för hela befolkningen 15–74 år, AKU Fjärde kvartalet 2016, scb.se, February 14, 2017

Employment rates among low-skilled immigrants were far lower than those of native Swedes... *Finding the Way: A Discussion of the Swedish Migrant Integration System*, OECD, Paris, 2014

Seven years or for a new arrival to get work... A 2015 report for the Swedish government found that it too between 7 and 10 years for just 50 per cent of new arrivals to find a job. *Nyanländas etablering – är statens insatser effektiva?* RiR 2015:17, Riksrevisionen, Stockholm, 2017

Stefan Löfven, "Sweden is at a crossroads..." Speech in Stockholm on February 29, 2016: "Striden om den svenska modellen", socialdemokraterna.se

"A grenade under the Swedish model". Olof Svensson, "Kritiken: Annie Lööf driver en Sovjet-politik", aftonbladet.se, February 5, 2016

The typical Swedish way of solving problems is the pragmatic way..." The agreement on subsidised etableringsjobb was announced in March 2018.

Ek and Lorentzon's open letter: "Vi måste agera eller bli omsprungna!" medium.com/@SpotifySE, April 12, 2016

"It is almost impossible for immigrants and new arrivals to penetrate this market..." Quoted in David Crouch, "Pitfalls of rent restraints: why Stockholm's model has failed many", theguardian.com, August 19, 2015

The Housing Board's bombshell estimate: "Reviderad prognos över behovet av nya bostäder till 2025", boverket.se, June 2016

According to the Tenants Union... Lee Roden, "The story of Sweden's housing crisis", thelocal.se, August 28, 2017

Getting to the front of the line in central Stockholm takes 20 years... "Almost 580,000 now waiting for apartments in Stockholm", thelocal.se, August 16, 2017

Property prices rose six-fold in 20 years... See the chart provided by Eshe Nelson, "Sweden's cooling housing market is a preview for others with low rates and property bubbles", qz.com, November 25, 2017. The average debt-to-income ratio for households with mortgages was 338 per cent in September 2016, according to Sweden's central bank, while total household debt was 86 per cent of GDP.

"Historic" investment in more housing: "Stöd som ska gynna ökat bostadsbyggande", regering.se, March 24, 2017

"Let me put it this way..." Henrik Landelius quoted in "Sweden's housing shortage from a builder's perspective", sverigesradio.se, February 25, 2016

The forecast for 2018 was for a dip in construction... "Bostadsbyggandet kan nå en topp i år", boverket.se, November 9, 2017

228

In one school just two of its 750 pupils are classified as ethnic Swedish... Richard Milne, "Sweden immigration: Don't look back", FT.com, October 5, 2015

Groups like this were initially praised by politicians... I am thinking here primary of Hammenhög in southern Sweden, which was praised by the Migration Board and Conservative migration minister Tobias Billström in 2013 as a model for Sweden.

And there, more or less, its responsibility ends... Once an application for asylum has been accepted, refugees enter a formal, two-year integration programme, which includes language lessons and a reliable income

150,000 "good people": Marja Grill, Carolina Jemsby and Kenneth Ulander, "Dubbelt så många gode män än tidigare trott", svt.se, January 9, 2017

An absence of official statistics on ethnicity and crime... Lee Roden, "Why Sweden doesn't keep stats on ethnicity and crime", thelocal.se, May 8, 2018

That Daily Mail story: Nick Fagge, "EXCLUSIVE – The city destroyed by migration: Inside the Swedish town where armed gangs patrol the streets, crime has exploded and a beautiful social worker's murder has shocked Europe", dailymail.co.uk, January 30, 2016

I found people struggling to cope... David Crouch, "Gothenburg's refugee youths: 'Come and meet us – nobody is here to be violent'", theguardian.com, April 7, 2016

A spate of deadly, gang-related violence... David Crouch, "Sweden shooting puts focus on life in 'ghettoes without hope'", theguardian.com, March 20, 2015

More than 500 days to get a decision on asylum: "Avgjorda asylärenden beslutade av Migrationsverket, förstagångsansökningar, 2018", migrationsverket.se, May 1, 2018

The government cut its borrowing and debt fell... "Stort budgetöverskott 2017", riksgalden.se, January 9, 2018

Joakim Ruist's estimates: Joakim Ruist, Tid för Integration: Rapport till Expertgruppen för studier i offentlig ekonomi 2018:3, Regeringskansliet, Finansdepartementet, 2018

Trust in Sweden's institutions appears to be rising... "Resultat från SOM-seminariet 2018", som.gu.se, April 25, 2018

Andreas Johansson Heinö, "Flyktingarna orsakade inte någon tillitskollaps", bt.se, April 29, 2018

Many of those who argue for tight limits on immigration... The locus classicus is David Goodhart's 2004 article "Discomfort of strangers", reprinted on theguardian.com, February 24, 2004

500,000 new staff over the next 10 years... Sveriges viktigaste jobb finns i välfärden: Rekryteringsrapport 2018, Sveriges Kommuner och Landsting, Stockholm, 2018

The Gunnar Myrdal quote is from the condensed version of his 1,500-page report, published as The Negro in America, first issued in 1948. My edition was published in 1964 by Harper Torchbooks, New York, and the quote is on pages 318–319

Chapter 6: View from the top

Interviews with a Wallenberg are like hen's teeth... Books on the Wallenberg family include Ronald Fagerfjäll, "To Move From The Old To What Is About To Come Is The Only Tradition Worth Keeping", Investor, Stockholm, 2016; and David Bartal, The Empire: The Rise of the House of Wallenberg. Dagens Industry, Stockholm, 1996

"We work our butts off in the financial part..." Interviewed by Richard Milne, "The Wallenbergs: where money meets Swedish science", FT.com, February 14, 2017

"The country has a disproportionate number of world-leading, high-tech companies in relation to the number of citizens..." In the decade from 2005, Stockholm developed more billion-dollar tech companies than any other city in Europe. On a per-capita basis, Stockholm is the second most prolific tech hub globally, with 6.3 billion-dollar companies per million people compared to Silicon Valley with 6.9, according to a 2015 study by Atomico. Atomico is a technology investment firm based in London and founded by Niklas Zennström, who co-founded Skype. See, for example, Murad Ahmed, "Stockholm: the unicorn factory", FT.com. March 31, 2015. In 2018, Sweden topped the Inc. 5000 list as the European country with the fastest-growing private companies.

229

Fredrik Reinfeldt: "The Swedish people want the Swedish model..." Interviewed by John Thornhill, "How the 'nasty party' can defy Juncker's curse", FT.com, September 15, 2008

Chapter 7: 'Freeing the Tiger'
Links to much of the material about the Asphalt Indians is still present on their defunct website, https://asfaltsdjungelnsindianer.wordpress.com/

They wrote in a popular newspaper... Asfalts-djungelns indianer, "Ditt lyxåk kör miljön i botten", aftonbladet.se, August 13, 2007

"The target has been to find a design that is not as 'macho' as that of many other SUV models..." The quote is in: "Volvo ACC concept car – first-class SUV challenger", media.volvocars.com, January 8, 1997

SUVs were intrinsically "dangerous, thirsty and heavy"... Alla Bilar 2003 magazine, quoted in Olle Hagman and Martin Bae Pedersen, 'How Big Became Bad The Breakthrough and Stigma-tization of 'City Jeeps' in Sweden, 1984–2007", ICON, 16, 2010, pp143–158

Sweden's fleet of cars was "worst in class"... Per Kågeson, "Reducing CO2 Emissions from New Cars: A progress report on the car industry's vol-untary agreement and an assessment of the need for policy instruments", European Federation for Transport and Environment, Brussels, 2005

"Please let me try. It is my dream...." Quoted in "Li Shufu", chinadaily.com.cn, March 27, 2006

Volvo could give him the innovation, branding and technology he needed... Pedro Nueno and Gary Liu, "How Geely waited for Volvo," FT.com, December 19, 2011

Like "a world famous movie star marrying a peasant in China"... As above.

"The Chinese car industry is primitive..." Jacques Wallner, "Kineserna har inget att lära Saab och Volvo", dn.se, September 9, 2009

"Geely can kill Volvo's strengths..." Lasse Swärd, "Geely kan döda Volvos styrkor", dn.se, December 5, 2009

Sundemo: jobs will move out of Sweden... "Geelys intresse väcker oro", svd.se, September 9, 2009

Unlisted companies in the Caymans... "Facket vill att Geely ska granskas", dn.se, December 9, 2009

Sören Gyll quote: "Gyll kämpar för Volvo PV", GP.se, September 27, 2009

Löfven's quotes on Geely: "Svenska budgivare ger inte upp", GP.se, October 28, 2009

Li Shufu, "Geely is Geely and Volvo is Volvo..." "Li Shufu, CV and Biography", media.volvocars.com, July 15, 2010

Li Shufu, "We gave them back their freedom." Quoted in Richard Milne and Christian Shepherd, "Volvo: Remaking the marque", FT.com, June 19, 2016

"In 2010, it took Volvo 44 months to develop a new car..." As above.

Christer Karlsson is quoted in ibid.

Gyllenhammar quotes: Karin Olander, "Jag tycker att man har förstört hela Volvo", weekend.di.se, July 14, 2016

"The feeling among senior Volvo executives..." Jessica Twentyman, "Volvo's digital launch of the XC90 marks 'connected car' era", FT.com, December 8, 2015

"We have taken a step into the premium league..." Peter Campbell, "Volvo Cars' profits driven by demand for SUVs", FT.com, May 4, 2016

On Clotaire Rapaille, see for example Hagman and Pedersen, above.

Stephen Graham, Cities under Siege: The New Urban Militarism. London, Verso, 2011

Li Khufu, "too Scandinavian": quoted in Milne and Shepherd, see above

Chapter 8: Paved with good intentions
On Noah's plans for Brevik: "NOAH vurderer videre farlig avfallsavfallsbehandling på Langøya etter at deponiet er fullt", noah.no, September 17, 2017

On the potential risks to local residents: Øyvind Lie, "Planlegger gigantisk deponi for farlig avfall et steinkast unna boligområde", tu.no, October 21, 2015

Regarding Sweden's green reputation, you cannot get any more gushing than this: "If there's a paradise for environmentalists, this Nordic nation of 9.2 million people must be it." Gwladys Fouché, "Sweden's carbon-tax solution to climate change puts it top of the green list", theguardian.com, April 29, 2008

More than half the energy Sweden generates is from renewable sources... says the official web-site of Sweden, sweden.se/quick-facts

Facebook consumes more than one per cent of Sweden's total energy production, a proportion set to double... "Facebook effect turns Swedish steel town into tech hot-spot", af.reuters.com, May 7, 2018

On the 1972 UN environment conference in Stockholm: Richard Black, "Stockholm: Birth of the green generation," bbc.com, June 4, 2012

Greenhouse gas emissions but by a quarter while the economy has grown 60 per cent: "When It Comes to Emissions, Sweden Has Its Cake and Eats It Too", worldbank.org, May 16, 2016

The the tax on nitrogen oxide emissions: Lena Höglund-Isaksson and Thomas Sterner, "Innovation Effects of the Swedish NOX Charge", OECD Global forum on Eco-innovation, Paris, November 4-5, 2009

Sweden's climate agreement breaks the pattern of short-termism... Anders Wijkman, "Historiskt klimatbeslut", hagainitiativet.se, June 15, 2017

Wijkman's quote "Since the 1980s, capitalism has moved from furthering..." is from Ernst Ulrich von Weizsäcker and Anders Wijkman, Come On! Capitalism, Short-termism, Population and the Destruction of the Planet: A Report to the Club of Rome, Springer, New York, 2018, page 2

Short-term incentives are needed to reward long-term action... As above, page 96

The history of district heating in Sweden: Bengt Johansson et al, The Use of Biomass for Energy in Sweden: Critical Factors and Lessons Learned. Report 35, Lund University Department of Energy and Environmental System Studies, 2002

Sweden's Climate Act: Akshat Rathi, "Sweden legally commits to reaching net-zero emissions by 2045", qz.com, June 16, 2017

Hybrit is a collaboration between private Swedish steel company SSAB, publicly owned iron ore miner LKAB, and public utility Vattenfall, backed by the state in the shape of the Swedish Energy Agency, Energimyndigheten

Conclusion: The new Swedish model

Everything I know about the life of the bumble-bee is thanks to Dave Goulson, A Sting in the Tale: My Adventures with Bumblebees, 2013, Jonathan Cape

On the measurement of bumblebee flight: Michael Dickinson, "Le vol des insectes", pourlascience.fr, August 1, 2001; Douglas L. Altshuler et al, "Short-amplitude high-frequency wing strokes determine the aerodynamics of honeybee flight," Proceedings of the National Academy of Sciences, Vol. 102, No.50, 2005, pp.18213-18218

The term "new Swedish model" has been around for a while. For example: Dimitris Tsarouhas, Social Democracy in Sweden: The Threat from a Globalised World, I. B. Tauris, 2008

"Sweden is proof that regulated capitalism..." This observation has been made eloquently by the eminent Swedish political scientist Bo Rothstein: "Politikens höger-vänster har börjat spela ut sin roll", dn.se, May 20, 2017. The experi-ence of Macron in power suggests that he leans to the right in his economic preferences.

That Economist special report: Adrian Wool-dridge, "The next supermodel: politicians from both right and left could learn from the Nordic countries," special report on the Nordic countries, The Economist, February 2, 2013

When asked what the Swedish model stood for in 2012... Demoskop, "Den svenska välfärden: Allmänhetens om framtida utmaningarna och möjligheterna", presented at Almedalen, July 5, 2012

INTERVIEWS

Andersson, Kristian, *HR director, Volvo AB*

Andersson, Mats, *financier and asset manager, former CEO, Fourth Swedish National Pension Fund (AP4)*

Bennet, Carl, *Getinge AB*

Berggren, Henrik, *Palme's biographer*

Bergström, Glenn, *IF Metall representative on Volvo Cars board*

Borg, Anders, *former finance minister*

Braunerhjelm, Pontus, *Professor, KTH*

Brzezinski, Natalia, *CEO, Stockholm Symposium*

Carlén, Thomas, *economist, LO*

Cerruti, Paulo, *COO, Northvolt*

Duvander, Ann-Zofie, *Professor, Department of Sociology, Stockholm University*

Ehrensvärd, Stina, *CEO Yubico*

Einarsson, Petra, *CEO Sandvik Materials Technology,*

Enocson, Hans, *outgoing CEO for GE in Sweden*

Eskilsson, Henrik, *CEO Tobii Group*

Ferbe, Anders, *head of IF Metall*

Forseke, Karin, *former CEO, Carnegie Bank*

Forssell, Johan, *Investor CEO*

Forster, Carl-Peter, *Volvo Cars*

Godner, Boel, *mayor of Södertälje*

Graham, Stuart, *former CEO, Skanska*

Hallqvist, Bo, *City Development Administration*
Hedberg, Pär, *CEO, Stockholm Innovation and Growth*

Hedman, Per-Oscar, *press manager Fortum Group Sweden, and Kristoffer Elblaus, operations manager*

Hedström, Lennart, *TRR*

Hugusson, Bjorn, *klimatchef, Stockholm City*

Johnstone, Tom, *former CEO, SKF*

Johannson, Leif, *chairman AstraZeneca*

Joyce, Patrick, *Ratio Institute*

Kerssemakers, Lex, *Volvo Cars board*

Leten, Ronnie, *former CEO, Atlas Copco*

Lindvall, Johannes, *Professor, Lund University*

Lundgren, Kurt, *author of Landet Lagom*

Malström, Anders, *Glue*

McLoughlin, Keith, *former CEO, Electrolux*

Mehks, Janey, *Invest Stockholm*

Mitchell, Linnéa, *yoga teacher*

Moberg, Anders, *IKEA*

Mogren, Håkan, *Investor Board*

Nordmark, Eva, *head of TCO*

Persson, Göran, *former prime minister*

Raffelsberger, Hanna, *Gunnebo Gateway*

Rankka, Maria, *recently CEO, Stockholm Chamber of Commerce*

Ruist, Joakim, *Professor, Gothenburg University*

Saadeha, Ahmad, *IT business analyst, Volvo AB*

Sandgren, Johan, *TRR*

Stenberg, Erik, *Professor, KTH*

Stenebo, Johan, *former IKEA CEO*

Stensson, Gunilla *(not her real name)*

Sundemo, Magnus, *Volvo unions*

Thorwarldsson, Karl-Petter, *head of LO*

Twomey, Richard, *CEO Molnlycke Healthcare*

Wahlroos, Björn, *CEO, Nordea*

Walerud, Jane, *angel investor*

Wallenberg, Jacob, *Chairman, Investor*

Walter, Lars, *Professor, School of Business, Economics and Law, Gothenburg University*

Weihe, Anders, *chief economist for the engineering employers federation, Teknikföretagen*

Zhang, Peter, *Volvo Cars board*

Åman, Marina, *head of Unionen*

233

234

David Crouch

British freelance journalist David Crouch moved
to Sweden in August 2013, settling in Gothenburg on the west coast. Previously he was a
news editor at the *Financial Times* in London.
Reporting mainly for the *Guardian*, he also
teaches investigative journalism at Gothenburg
university and works in corporate communications. In a previous life, he acquired a D.Phil.
in the sociology of scientific knowledge. In
another previous life, he was a writer and editor
in Moscow.

Tina Axelsson

Swedish photographer and filmmaker Tina
Axelsson is known for her portraits, reportage,
album covers, dance and fashion work. During
a career spanning more than 20 years, her
curiosity for people and cultures has taken her
around the globe. Says a colleague who became
a friend: "Tina is wild at heart. She has an ability to
capture the essence of a person that is intimate
and even philosophical." She lives with her family
in Stockholm.

Acknowledgements

This was a good idea for a book. I wish it had
been mine. I am indebted to Tor Bonnier and
Mats Bergstrand for realising that someone
needed to write about the Swedish model from
a business perspective, and then choosing me to
do it and covering my expenses. I am grateful to
Mats for his excellent connections to the movers
and shakers in Swedish society, and also to his
insistence that I should maintain journalistic independence over this project. How I carried it out
is entirely my responsibility. Many people have
given their time to help create this book, not
least those who agreed to be interviewed, and
the people who helped arrange those interviews.
Special thanks are due to Heather Farmbrough,
Eric Zsiga, Peter Jervelycke Belfrage, Camilla and
Steve Flood, and Orla Vigsø for editorial insight
and painstaking corrections, to Karin Wallström
Nordén for allowing me the flexibility to fit this
project around my other work commitments, to
Mikael Engblom for going the extra mile, and to
Tina Axelsson for sunshine. Annika shared the
highs and the lows (but mainly the lows), and
never lost faith.